Praise for

The Most Loving Place in Town

"This is a great story. Jesus placed all His bets on the mastering of love by His people. Read it—and get to work!"

—John Ortberg
Pastor, Menlo Park Presbyterian Church; and Author,
When the Game Is Over, It All Goes Back in the Box

"Only authors who love a church could have written such a beautiful parable. I was convicted as I identified with the characters. I was tremendously blessed as I saw God's plan for all churches. My eyes watered a few times, and my heart was filled with joy as I saw the church revived through sharing the love of Christ."

—Charles "Tremendous" Jones
Publisher, Executive Books

"In *The Most Loving Place in Town*, Ken Blanchard and Phil Hodges have showed us how *love* can, and must, transform us and the church. This is a must-read. But more importantly, it is a must *do* for every Christian and every church if we are truly to be followers of Jesus."

—Marjorie Dorr
Former Chief Strategy Officer, WellPoint

"With all the busyness and stress in our world today, this simple yet profoundly powerful story is a beacon of hope not only for church life but also for all of our lives. It's a call to remember that *God is love*, and we're called by Him to model that in every way that we live our lives, especially in His church. With leadership founded on Biblical *love*—not judgment, self-interest, or a plethora of programs—churches can begin to draw people back into the fold. This heartfelt book is the godly how-to handbook to do just that!"

—Barbara A. Glanz
Speaker and Author, *The Simple Truths of Service*, *The Simple Truths of Appreciation*, and *What Can I Do? Ideas to Help Those Who Have Experienced Loss*

"This is a must-read for everyone who claims to be a Christian. The book furnishes thought-provoking study questions that all church board members should use as a guide to examine themselves and the churches they are leading. Thank you, Ken and Phil, for reminding us of God's charge for our lives and the power of prayer."

—Roger Roberson
Chairman, Roberson Management

"We all know a thousand ways that the local church can fail. This book shows one way—the essential way—for the local church to succeed in carrying out its mission: become the most loving place in town. This book does for the local church what *Lead Like Jesus* does for the individual leader: it shows a way to make Jesus smile!"

—Greg Bunch
President, Masterplan International Corporation

"Ken and Phil have done it again! They keep hitting the center cut of the target! You'll want to pick up this new book and will not be able to put it down. God has truly blessed them with incredible gifts. You'll be blessed!

—Jim Blanchard
Retired Chairman and CEO, Synovus Financial Corp.

"*The Most Loving Place in Town* touches the very sorest place in the human heart: our deep longing for a community of true kindness and grace. Ken Blanchard and Phil Hodges have written a moving and biblically sure-footed parable that will guide you and your congregation back to 'your first love.' Read this book, shed tears of repentance and joy, and make yourself available to the work God wants to do to renew love and caring in your local church."

—Ken Jennings and John Stahl-Wert
Best-Selling Authors, *The Serving Leader* and
Ten Thousand Horses

"*The Most Loving Place* reminds us that even though the busyness of Christ-centered communities is necessary, it is not primary. The business of those vibrant, living communities is *love*. We are reminded that choosing any action or activity over a loving relationship is a bad decision. With great insights and anecdotes, the authors remind us of three important truths: The best use of life is *love*. The best expression of love is *time*. And the best time to love is *now*."

—Mick Ukleja, PhD
President, Leadership Traq; and Best-Selling Author,
Who Are You and What Do You Want?

"It takes a couple of real servants to write a book about servant leadership and its number one ingredient: love. Ken and Phil do a great job of modeling the leadership style of Jesus. This book is a keeper on how it is done."

—C. Kemmons Wilson Jr.
Founding Family–Holiday Inns

"All of us earnestly desire to be in a loving church. However, many churches are not the most loving places in town. In this parable, Ken and Phil have shown us how to start the journey under the guidance of the Holy Spirit to transform our own church into the most loving place in town."

—Micky Blackwell
Former President and COO, Lockheed Martin
Aeronautical Systems

"This book takes us back to basics: love God, and love one another. The parable brings to life the simple yet profound truths that Jesus taught through His deeds and words. Churches that embrace the message of this book can become the most loving places in town."

—Bobby Ukrop
President and CEO, Ukrop's Super Markets, Inc.

"In the engaging narrative style that has become a hallmark of Ken Blanchard and Phil Hodges, *The Most Loving Place in Town* is the perfect remedy for anyone in any environment—whether church, business, or home—who has developed 'spiritual cataracts.' This book should find its way into the hands of every churchgoer in the nation— better yet, in the world!"

—Paul J. Meyer
Founder, Success Motivation International, Inc.,
and *New York Times* Best-Selling Author

THE MOST LOVING
PLACE IN TOWN

THE MOST LOVING PLACE IN TOWN

A MODERN-DAY PARABLE FOR THE CHURCH

Ken Blanchard & Phil Hodges

THOMAS NELSON

Since 1798

NASHVILLE   DALLAS   MEXICO CITY   RIO DE JANEIRO

Published in Nashville, Tennessee, by Thomas Nelson. Thomas Nelson is a trademark of Thomas Nelson, Inc.

Page design by Mandi Cofer.

Thomas Nelson, Inc. titles may be purchased in bulk for educational, business, fund-raising, or sales promotional use. For information, please e-mail SpecialMarkets@ThomasNelson.com.

This parable is a work of fiction. Names, characters, places, and incidents are either products of the authors' imagination or used fictitiously. All characters are fictional, and any similarity to people living or dead is purely coincidental.

Unless otherwise noted, Scripture quotations are taken from the Holy Bible: New International Version®. © 1973, 1978, 1984 by International Bible Society. Used by permission of Zondervan Publishing House. All rights reserved.

Scripture quotations noted NKJV are from the New King James Version®. © 1982 by Thomas Nelson, Inc. Used by permission. All rights reserved.

Scripture quotations noted ESV are from the English Standard Version. © 2001 by Crossway Bibles, a division of Good News Publishers.

ISBN 978-0-8499-4704-9 (trade paper)

Library of Congress Cataloging-in-Publication Data

Blanchard, Kenneth H.
   The most loving place in town : a modern-day parable for the church / Ken Blanchard and Phil Hodges.
      p. cm.
   ISBN 978-0-7852-2893-6 (hardcover)
   1. Church. I. Hodges, Phil. II. Title.
   BV600.3.B53 2008
   253—dc22

                              2008024714

Printed in the United States of America
10 11 12 13 14 QW 6 5 4 3 2 1

"By this all men will know that you are my disciples, if you love one another."

—JOHN 13:35

CONTENTS

Contents

ACKNOWLEDGMENTS

Ken and Phil thank their wives, Margie and Jane, for their loving support on the journey to *The Most Loving Place in Town*. They also extend their gratitude to Phyllis Hendry for her loving leadership of the Lead Like Jesus ministries.

Ken has been blessed by fabulous colleagues in The Ken Blanchard Companies. The concepts that they taught him appear throughout this book. He would like to thank Jesse Stoner, his coauthor on *Full Steam Ahead!*, for her pioneering work in visioning and Pat Zigarmi, coauthor of *Leading at a Higher Level*, for the research she was involved in around the concerns people have during change.

Phil thanks Karen McGuire and Martha Lawrence for

their encouragement, wisdom, editorial support, and love for the book. He also thanks Micky Blackwell for his insightfulness on corporate prayer. For their willingness to provide suggestions and insights on the work, Phil thanks Kathy McKinnie, Owen Phelps, Greg Bunch, Sally and Steve Patay, and Bruce Humphries. Phil also thanks the real Golden Oldies—Harley Damon, Vergil Best, and Phil Seitz—his accountability partners for the past fifteen years. For their unconditional love, Phil thanks the Hodges and Pinner families, especially his grandchildren, Julia, John, James, Philip, Sarah, and Samuel. Finally, he sends a special thank-you to his late mother, Elizabeth Hodges, the woman who taught him about unconditional love.

Chapter 1

THE LETTER

"Thank the Lord for term limits," Tim Manning muttered to himself as he looked down at the agenda from last night's meeting of the Beacon Hill Community Church Elder Council. Three months from finishing his third consecutive two-year term as church chairman, Tim was ineligible to serve a fourth term. Although ambivalent about leaving office, he had to admit that it was good that he go. He still cared passionately about the church and was gratified by many things that had happened during his term in office. But he was worn out. After eighty-two council meetings, twenty-three congregational business meetings, and countless daily phone calls, e-mails, and coffee-shop meetings, he was ready to turn over leadership responsibilities to the next "suffering servant."

Tim had no idea that his most important leadership journey with the church would begin in a matter of moments.

As Tim reviewed the agenda, he paused at the third item: "Beacon Hill 30th Anniversary Celebration—Planning Update." It was a bit unusual to hold a thirtieth anniversary celebration. But his predecessor had abruptly shelved plans for a twenty-fifth anniversary celebration when the head pastor was fired for participating in local demonstrations against the war. The extreme tension that had permeated the church at that time precluded any attempts at joyful celebration.

In the aftermath, attendance had dropped. There was a significant loss of financial support when some long-term members left the church over the pastor's firing. Budget talks became competitive, contentious, and sometimes downright nasty.

As the new incoming chairman, Tim, along with the rest of the leadership team, had spent a lot of time and effort to prevent an out-and-out split in the church. Emotions ran high. Walls went up between the opposing sides of the decision to fire the pastor. When the furor calmed down, cold politeness froze over an undercurrent of deep anger and hurt. It had been a time of testing that brought Tim to his knees, asking God for the patience and wisdom not to respond out of his own pride, fear, and frustration.

With the passage of time and the departure of some of the more bitter members of the congregation, the church slowly began to heal. The arrival of Mike Reston, a gifted young pastor with clear doctrine and an engaging preaching style, further buoyed up the spirits of the congregation. When an auto parts plant opened nearby, an influx of new people into the area gradually restored weekend attendance to former levels. Giving increased with the turnaround in the stock market, and the health of the balance sheet vastly improved.

Today Tim believed that the church was again strong. It was certainly buzzing with activity. Something was going on every night. Bible studies, support groups, commission meetings, and the annual surges of activity centered on the Christmas and Easter pageants left little time for idle hands. There had been such a positive change that Tim gladly had endorsed the idea to hold the Beacon Hill Community Church thirtieth anniversary celebration in the coming year.

As he thought about it, Tim could look back on a season of leadership when working hard, persevering, and keeping the gospel message alive and on track had borne fruit. He even secretly pictured himself receiving a "well done, good and faithful servant" for his efforts. He smiled and reviewed the rest of the agenda:

♥ Review of requests by three ministry commissions for improved funding in next year's budget

- ♥ Recommendations from the Finance and Property Commission on delaying the reroofing of the Christian education building

- ♥ Open discussion on how to better deal with the number of marriages in crisis

- ♥ Results of negotiations between the leaders of the New Horizon Senior Sunday School Class and student ministries on switching meeting rooms

- ♥ Plans for the National Day of Prayer

It contained the usual set of land mines but nothing Tim hadn't been able to handle. He had to admit that he had come down pretty hard on one of the younger elders who had suggested a delay in beginning the reroofing project. This was something Tim had his heart set on completing before his term of office was over. By the end of last night's meeting— after lots of active and sometimes heated conversations—all the issues had been resolved, and everyone had left in a good humor, more or less.

Just three more months of council meetings. Tim wondered what it would be like to have every other Tuesday night back. No more hurried suppers, over-the-speed-limit dashes to the church, and those wide-awake debriefings that delayed sleep and made Wednesday mornings at work a real challenge.

He noted that he would dearly miss the fellowship, devotional teaching, and prayer time that he shared with his fellow elders. Again, Tim smiled. He cared about these folks. As a group, including himself, they were not perfect. But God love them, they came together twice a month at the end of a hard day of working out in the world to do their best about God's business. They prayed together, laughed together, fought with each other, and by God's grace made their share of good, great, and not-so-great decisions together.

Still, Tim was looking forward to taking some time off with a sense of a job well done.

Feeling satisfied, Tim put aside the agenda and thumbed through the morning mail. His eyes went immediately to a handwritten envelope addressed to Tim Manning, BHCC Chairman. Usually items addressed to him in this manner contained one of two things—a complaint from a member of the congregation or, on rare occasions, a note of encouragement. He wondered what it would be this time.

The single sheet was written in a clear but unfamiliar hand. It read:

Dear Tim,

I have been observing you and your season of leadership at Beacon Hill for many years and thought it important to write to you at this time. I have watched your hard work in guiding Beacon Hill out of a period of turmoil and challenge. You have endured a great deal and persevered with energy in creating a level of excitement and activity within the church. For all this I commend you and the other leaders who have worked with you.

Tim paused in his reading and thought, *Wow! I was just hoping to get a "well done, good and faithful servant," and here it is in this morning's mail.* He read on:

I'm writing to bring something important to your attention. You have lost your first love. You and Beacon Hill Community Church have drifted away from the love of God and one another as your first priority and into a pattern of success-driven busyness. If this serious situation is not turned around, it will destroy the church's credibility.

Fear not, Tim. All is not lost. I am writing to encourage you to lead a change that, under the guidance of the Holy Spirit, can be accomplished. If you accept the challenge to restore love into the life of the church by reviving the passion and humility that were present when the church was first starting out, you and Beacon Hill will receive blessings beyond your imagination. The way back must start with you.

This letter is sent in love as always, with faith that what is required can be done.

Your Truest Friend

Tim stared at the letter in disbelief. His thoughts quickly turned to frustration. While the writer had sugarcoated the feedback, Tim was convinced it came from one of the chronic critics he had learned to endure during his terms in office.

He frowned. "For ax grinders like this person, nothing is ever right," he said out loud. Silently he continued to rationalize.

Beacon Hill is far from being out of control, and a lot is being accomplished to further the kingdom, he thought. *The numbers have turned around in the church's giving and attendance. The people of this church share a common cause in doing things in the Lord's name. There's a new sense of urgency. Things are on the move again!*

With that off his chest, Tim tossed the letter into the wastebasket and began sorting through the rest of the mail. He always prided himself on keeping up with his regular mail as well as his e-mail. He was about to write some notes on the yellow legal pad he always kept at his desk when the phone rang.

Feeling mildly annoyed at the interruption, he answered with an abrupt "hello."

"Mr. Manning?" It was a woman's voice, and something in her tone told Tim this was not going to be good news.

Chapter 2

THE PHONE CALL

"Yes," Tim said into the receiver, a cautious tone in his voice. "Who's this?"

"I don't know if you remember me, but my name is Dani Wilson. You might remember—you prayed with me after Sunday service a couple of months ago when I was worried about a singing audition I had coming up."

Regaining his composure, Tim took a breath and said, "I remember you well, Dani, and your beautiful singing voice. How did the audition go?"

"Sorry to say, I didn't get the part, but our prayer was answered in a different way. I got a job waiting tables that will pay my bills until the next opportunity comes along. So, thanks."

Tim remembered Dani's sparkle. "It's great to hear from you!" he said warmly. "To what do I owe the honor of your call?"

"I don't know how much of an honor it is," said Dani. "But I wanted to let you know that I've decided to look for another church. I was going to leave without saying anything, but since you were so nice to me, I felt I should let you know."

Her announcement caught Tim by surprise. "I'm sorry to hear that," he said after a pause. "Would you mind telling me why you're leaving?"

"It's, uh, kind of a long story," Dani said with hesitation. "But I guess the bottom line is that Beacon Hill isn't exactly the most loving place in town."

With that comment, Tim's discounting of the handwritten letter he'd tossed in the wastebasket was coming into question.

"Dani, I'd like to understand what led you to that conclusion. I'd really appreciate the chance to hear you out," said Tim kindly. "Don't be afraid to tell me the unfiltered truth. I hear it on good authority that the truth will set us free," he added with a chuckle.

There was a long pause before Dani broke the silence. "Don't get me wrong," she began. "I know people work real hard to make Beacon Hill a great church. It's just not the place for me, I guess."

"And why is that?" Tim asked.

"What it comes down to is that going to church at Beacon Hill doesn't make me feel closer to God. No offense, but sometimes I go away from there feeling farther away from God than I did before I arrived."

Another long pause followed. Tim felt a surge of defensiveness. The idea crossed his mind that Dani's failure to connect might be her personal problem and not a reflection of the church. He was shocked by his knee-jerk rejection of any feedback and his eagerness to place the blame back on Dani. "Did anything in particular happen that made you feel . . . farther away from God after coming to church?" Tim asked.

Again, Dani was slow to answer. She finally continued, "It took me a long time to figure this out because it seems like the church is doing all the right things. The Bible teaching is good, the music during worship services is awesome, and there are an amazing number of programs and ministries. But somehow it feels like the activities are more important than God—or even the church members."

"Can you give me an example?"

"Sure. Following Pastor Mike's suggestion, I got involved in a small group. It wasn't a good experience. For one thing, it seemed like the leader was more interested in making sure we got through the lessons than sharing our hearts and connecting with each other. What really stuck in my mind was when one of the group members got down on me for the version of the Bible I was using. I felt more judged than loved."

This conversation was starting to feel heavy, but Tim pressed on. "Anything else?" he asked.

"When I volunteered to help out with the Christmas pageant, all I wanted to do was to serve God by making it the best pageant ever. I had so much enthusiasm at the beginning. But after a couple of weeks of being treated like I was a hired hand, I got discouraged. No one got back to me when I had questions or suggestions. And no one thanked me."

"I'm sorry to hear that," said Tim. He opened his mouth to say more, but before he could get a word out, Dani continued.

"It's ironic that the theme of the pageant was 'Season of Kindness,'" she said. "I really want my church to feel like a place where I'm welcome and where people are genuinely glad to see me. This may sound like I'm whining, but it seems like you have to be an established member to get that kind of love."

Her statement was so close to what the letter had implied that Tim was stunned. "Is there anything else?" he asked, hoping there wasn't.

"I understand that not everybody can be involved in the music ministry, but God gave me a gift, Mr. Manning. I've been singing since I was four. My biggest joy is sharing my gift with others. I would love church to be a place where I could praise and worship God in song. Unfortunately that's not going to happen at Beacon Hill."

"Why not?" Tim asked.

"I auditioned, and they told me I had a great voice, but nobody ever got back to me. I know things like this slip through the cracks, but I'm tired of being one of those 'things.'"

"I'm sorry to hear that," Tim said again, feeling like a broken record. "Look, on behalf of the church, I really want to apologize. But most of all I want to thank you for caring enough to give me this feedback. It hasn't been comfortable, but it's been valuable. I'm going to look into what you've said because I hope to create a church where you'll feel more than welcome. Can I talk you into coming back and giving us another chance?"

After a short silence, Dani said, "I'll think about it. You've been really nice. I appreciate your taking the time to hear me out."

After they said their good-byes, Tim hung up the phone and slowly sat back in his chair, settling into a contemplative mood. All his visions of a hero's recognition for his leadership efforts quickly dissolved with the one-two punch he'd just gotten from the anonymous letter followed by Dani's call. Retrieving the letter from the wastebasket, he reread: "You and Beacon Hill Community Church have drifted away from the love of God and one another." Those words, combined with Dani's comment that "Beacon Hill isn't exactly the most loving place in town," stabbed him right in the heart. Why?

Because he knew in his gut they were right. The church buzzed with activity, but much of the love was gone. When and how had it happened? Why hadn't he and the other leaders seen that the love was missing?

Tim read the letter again, more slowly this time. Having lowered his defenses, he noted a number of things during this reading. The writer commended and encouraged him before confronting him. Unlike many complaints he'd received, this letter contained a concise statement of the problem and a specific recommendation of what needed to be done to make things right. He also appreciated the clear warning about the consequences of inaction. This letter was written in both truth and love. Tim was thankful that it included the encouraging message, "All is not lost." The writer had a positive expectation that the church not only could be saved from disaster but, in fact, could be better than ever. Unfortunately, he didn't get that same feeling from Dani's call even though she, too, had shared her feelings in both truth and love.

Now what? Tim thought. With Pastor Mike still away on his two-month sabbatical and the pulpit filled with guest speakers, Tim knew one thing for sure: it would be up to him to lead the search for the love that was missing from Beacon Hill Community Church. He knew he could not do it alone. He would need help. *But where will that come from?* he wondered.

Glancing at the letter once again, Tim was drawn to one sentence in particular: "I am writing to encourage you to lead a change that, under the guidance of the Holy Spirit, can be accomplished."

"Under the guidance of the Holy Spirit," Tim repeated out loud. That made him smile.

He had been in his forties when he'd finally turned his life over to the Lord. At that time he was a senior manager of a manufacturing company. Before he finally surrendered, a pastor friend had said to him, "Tim, I don't know why you haven't signed up a lot sooner. After all, you get three consultants for the price of one—the *Father*, who started it all and is *for you*, the *Son*, who lived it and is always *with you*, and the *Holy Spirit*, who is *in you* and is your day-to-day operating manager."

Tim hadn't thought much about the Holy Spirit in the last few years, but today he realized he could certainly use a day-to-day operating manager on his side.

Chapter 3

LOVE LOST

With his wife, Linda, out of town caring for her ailing mother, Tim was home alone that evening with his thoughts about what to do to bring love—of God and one another—back into the church.

He reasoned that if the church had drifted away from its first-love priority, he had to assume much of the responsibility. A wise saying often quoted by his mentor, Hank Dalton, came to mind: *When things don't work out the way you have planned, it is better to look in the mirror and ask, "What more could I have done?" rather than look out the window to find someone else to blame.*

Instead of looking elsewhere to lay the blame, Tim, with faith in his all-forgiving Savior, bowed his head in prayer.

"Lord Jesus, forgive me for drifting away from You and making my leadership more about getting things done than about loving You. Help me find the way back to making loving You and my brothers and sisters my leadership priority. Lord, I surrender my heart to You so You can set it on the right path."

Having taken the first step to rekindle his first-love priority, Tim realized he'd need a clear vision of what to restore in the church before he could invite other people into the process. It was still hard to accept that with all that he saw as right about the church, something so wrong had happened. To make sure his old enemies of fear, pride, and denial wouldn't take over, Tim grabbed his Bible, a pen, and one of his yellow legal pads and took a seat at the kitchen table.

As he often did, Tim went to his Bible to seek God's perspective on the issue. He opened the book to Paul's celebrated description of love in 1 Corinthians 13:1–3 (NKJV) and read:

Though I speak with the tongues of men and of angels, but have not love, I have become sounding brass or a clanging cymbal.

And though I have the gift of prophecy, and understand all mysteries and all knowledge, and though I have all faith, so that I could remove mountains, but have not love, I am nothing.

And though I bestow all my goods to feed the

poor, and though I give my body to be burned, but have not love, it profits me nothing.

Tim sighed. He realized the lost love at Beacon Hill was real. As he thought about it, relationships at the church had drifted into patterns of low-grade rivalries and silos of interest in different parts of the ministry. The focus on filling the calendar with special events and activities had brought about increased competition for resources between people passionate about their favorite part of the ministry. There had been occasional flare-ups of old anger and deep wounds that still kept some people at arm's length from one another. Tim also had to admit that he had grown complacent about the condition of the church once the finances had improved and attendance had been restored.

Tim picked up his pen and began to write down his initial thoughts about the problem he was facing:

At Beacon Hill, we've lost sight of loving God and one another as our defining priority. We have drifted into celebrating the work of the church instead of being a love-centered community. We have cherished efficiency and excellence at the expense of encouraging and nurturing our relationships. We seem to have forgotten that we find our reason for being a church in our loving relationship with Jesus.

Tim made a final note:

What's been lost:
The love that unites and defines us.

How could the love that had been lost in the church be restored? Again it crossed Tim's mind that the problem was bigger than he could solve on his own. He needed help from someone he could trust. He picked up the phone and dialed the familiar number of his friend and mentor, Hank Dalton. After a brief chat, Tim arranged to visit Hank the next day.

Later that night, Tim made his nightly call to Linda, who was at her mother's house. After hearing the daily report on her mom's condition, Tim poured out the events of his day. In the steady and encouraging manner he had come to rely on during the twenty-eight years of their marriage, Linda affirmed Tim's decision to seek Hank's advice.

"I love you, Linda," Tim said as they concluded their call.

"Love you too," she replied.

Early in their marriage, Linda's mom had advised them to keep their *I love you* up-to-date. They'd been heeding that advice, whether they were together or apart, for nearly three decades now.

Settling under the covers, Tim thought that if he had kept his *I love you* up-to-date with God, things at the church might have turned out differently.

Dani's words still haunted him as he drifted off to sleep: *Beacon Hill isn't exactly the most loving place in town.*

When he woke in the middle of the night, Tim's mind went right back to the problem at hand. So he might fall back asleep, he got up and wrote down some key points from the day:

- ♥ When things don't work out the way you have planned, it is better to look in the mirror and ask, "What more could I have done?" than to look out the window to find someone else to blame.

- ♥ God can change a surrendered heart and set it on the right path.

- ♥ It's a good idea to keep your *I love you* up-to-date.

Chapter 4

BLIND SPOTS REVEALED

On his way over to Hank's house the next morning, Tim realized that more time had passed than he would like to admit since he and Hank had spoken. Ever since Hank suffered some serious medical conditions and Tim's travel schedule increased, the pattern of their long-standing times of weekly fellowship and accountability had been broken.

Tim recalled how Hank, a former church chairman, and two other seasoned leaders had come alongside him when he was just starting out as church chairman. They invited him into a safe harbor fellowship of weekly breakfast meetings at a local restaurant. Because of his work schedule, "the Golden Oldies," as Tim's wife called them, agreed to start meeting at 6:30 a.m.

so he could make it to work by 8:00 a.m. His heart was touched anew by how much these meetings had meant to him when the pressures of leadership were bearing down on him. During those times, he had felt isolated. People weren't always honest with him, either because they wanted to please him or because they felt their agendas were more important. Truth-tellers were few and far between. Tim loved the fact that no matter what the topic of discussion, the Golden Oldies were straight shooters. If he was off base, they would tell him, and he would do the same for them. He reflected that if there were a starting point of his lost love priority, it may have been when the pattern of weekly accountability and fellowship stopped.

When he arrived at Hank's house, Tim laid out the whole story of the mysterious letter and handed Hank a copy. Tim went on to describe his phone call with Dani and her feelings of getting the cold shoulder from the church.

"I opened the Bible to 1 Corinthians 13, where I read that without love, all our efforts are basically pointless. You know, Hank," Tim said with a sigh, "it really hurts to think that things got so far off course on my watch. Now I'm afraid that there isn't enough time to put things right before my term is over. Frankly, I'm at a loss to know where to start."

After listening intently, Hank said, "One place we could start is to read the next paragraph of 1 Corinthians 13, which gives us a blueprint for love." Hank quoted from memory, "'Love is patient, love is kind. It does not envy, it does not boast, it is not proud. It is not rude, it is not self-seeking, it is not easily angered, it keeps no record of wrongs. Love does not delight in evil but rejoices with the truth. It always protects, always trusts, always hopes, always perseveres' [vv. 4–7]."

"That says it all," Tim admitted. "It's exactly what Dani described was missing from our church."

"Tim, when you were talking about the letter, you said, 'It really hurts to think that things got so far off course.' What is the 'it' that is hurting?"

Tim was quiet as he processed the question. Then he remembered it wasn't the first time he had been asked that question. In fact, it was one of the perennial questions that went around the breakfast table when the Golden Oldies challenged each other.

He smiled sheepishly and replied, "Just like old times, Hank, the 'it' is my pride. When I first read the letter, my thoughts went straight to what people would think of me if the word got out that they had been led astray. In a moment of weakness, my first thought was to keep the letter a secret and try to fix things without letting anybody know what I was doing."

"Sounds like you were having a David and Uriah the Hittite moment," said Hank with a knowing smile.

The image of the shepherd king trying to cover up his misdeeds with Bathsheba and getting deeper and deeper into trouble flashed into Tim's mind.

"You're right," he said. "But at least when I got that call from Dani and realized how she'd been hurt by the church, I let an old friend like you in on the situation to help put things in perspective."

"Glad to be of help," replied Hank. "What is your next move?"

"I don't really know," said Tim. "I think I've developed some kind of spiritual cataract that's caused me to lose sight of how to lead this church on the right path. I hoped you might have some suggestions on where I can go to bring love back to the church."

"Let me give that some thought," responded Hank. "I have a doctor's appointment this afternoon. Then under the watchful eye of my dear wife, I will be heavily engaged in my mandatory nap until about four. How about meeting back here when you get home from work?"

"Sounds great," Tim agreed. "I'll be here around five thirty."

Tim took some time that day to look up what Scripture had to say about love. There were literally hundreds of verses describing love, but the one that took his breath away was in Psalm 118, which stated:

His love endures forever.

It dawned on Tim that God's love for him had already endured every sin he had ever committed as well as every leadership miscue he had made. God's love for him burned with the same intensity that it always had and would endure forever. Tim was suddenly desperately hungry to respond in the most loving way he could and offered up a silent prayer.

AS HE WALKED up Hank's driveway at 5:30, Tim heard the sound of music that he always associated with his mentor. Looking in the window, he saw Hank seated at the piano, playing an old hymn, "Oh, How He Loves You and Me." Tim recognized it as one of Hank's favorites. It brought back fond memories of church functions in days gone by, when Hank entertained the church family with his lively playing and singalong talents. Tim hesitated before ringing the doorbell so he could drink in a little more of the sweetness of the sounds and the sight of his friend enjoying the soul satisfaction of making music.

Moments later when Hank responded to his delayed ringing of the doorbell, Tim remarked, "Sounds great, Hank. It's been a while since I've heard you tickling the ivories."

"I'm more than a little rusty," explained Hank. "Ever since my last two go-rounds with the doctors, I haven't felt much like playing. But it did feel good to get back at it after such a long time. I forgot how much I enjoy it. I think your call and our discussion this morning helped get some of my mental juices flowing again. While I was playing a few scales, trying to remind my fingers where to go on the keyboard, it occurred to me that maybe your focus on the 'doing' part of church leadership has caused you to become a little rusty on the 'being' part of the position."

"Tell me more," Tim encouraged him.

"Instead of telling you more, let me ask you a few questions that might highlight what I'm getting at," said Hank. "Remember our Monday morning accountability rule: 'a moment of brutal honesty is worth years of self-deception,'" he added with a smile.

"Fire away," replied Tim.

"Okay," said Hank. "Question one: When was the last time you went fly-fishing?" Hank had a twinkle in his eye as he waited for Tim's answer.

"Fly-fishing?" responded Tim. "What does that have to do with what we're talking about?"

"You'll see in a minute. But how about if I ask the questions and you give the answers?" replied Hank.

"Okay, you're the boss," said Tim. "Let's see. I think it's been over a year since I put a line in the water. With my travel schedule at work, the arrival of our first grandchild, and the usual load of church meetings and so forth, I just haven't had the time to get away for fly-fishing or, for that matter, for any other form of true downtime."

"Next question," said Hank. "How would you rate your prayer life today compared to six years ago when you were just starting out as church chairman? Hotter and more intense, colder and less frequent, or about the same?"

"Colder and less frequent, I guess," Tim admitted. "In the beginning, when I was stumbling around trying to figure out what to do, I was on my knees to God on a regular basis. When things started to turn around and I received some positive feedback on the way I was handling things, I started to drift away from daily time with God. Instead of seeking His guidance on where to go and what to do in His name, I edged into the habit of planning my course, asking Him to bless it or to help me out of trouble when things didn't go as I had planned."

"Question three," said Hank. "When you take time to get into God's Word, how do you most often approach the Scriptures—as a way to enrich your spiritual walk and relationship with Him or as a source of teaching material or validation of some position you have taken as chairman?"

"I know you have been laid up for a while," replied Tim, "so how did you keep up such intimate surveillance on my private habits?"

"No comment," said Hank. "Remember, I ask—you answer!"

"To tell you the truth, this has been a real struggle for me," answered Tim. "Preparing devotions for church meetings, researching scriptural responses to questions from the congregation, and participating in a weekly Bible study use up almost all of my time in the Word. It has become a rare day that I read the Bible for myself." Tim paused.

"These are pretty tough questions," he said with a weary smile. "Do you have any that I might actually enjoy answering?"

"Okay, friend, here's the last question," replied Hank. "When was the last time you felt God's unconditional love in your life?"

"Gee, Hank," said Tim, "that doesn't seem to be any easier a question to answer than the first ones."

"That depends on the answer," Hank stated.

"Well," said Tim, "I know and believe with all my heart that God loves me. But in all honesty, I talk about God's love and encourage others to believe and have faith in it more often than I feel it in my life. It's been a while since I felt like I did when I was a new believer, experiencing the passion and power of His love. I guess I've been using staying busy in work for the Lord as an excuse for not feeling as close to Him as I once did."

Tim added pensively, "Come to think of it, I'm a reflection of the kind of person the writer of the letter was describing—a person who has lost his first love. To put it in your terms, Hank, I have grown *rusty* in my walk with the Lord, and it has begun to show in my leadership at church. It probably has affected other aspects of my life as well. I just hope I can turn it around before I do any more damage."

"You have already started," observed Hank. "Remember

32

what the letter said—'All is not lost.' I know you can find the lost love with the help of the Holy Spirit," continued Hank, "because I've been on the same journey."

"You have?" replied Tim. "When was this?"

"Back when I was church chairman," recalled Hank. "Although I faced different practical problems than you have had in your term, I suffered some of the same symptoms of spiritual rustiness you have been describing.

"Just like your fly-fishing solitude, my early morning walks in the park and work in the garden became less and less frequent. My prayer time took on the nature of a to-do item in my daily planner so that I would not feel like too much of a hypocrite when I spoke to others about the power of prayer. My Bible reading became mechanical and a dry exercise of mental preparation rather than spiritual nourishment. I think the worst part of that time was the isolation I felt in trying to lead others when I wasn't sure of where I was headed."

"Really?" asked Tim. "What did you do to turn things around?"

"I redoubled my efforts to be more intentional about my walk with the Lord. I set new goals in my daily planner and announced my intentions to my wife so she could hold me accountable," said Hank.

"Then that's what I'll do," Tim said.

"Please don't," Hank urged him. "Because you'll notice all that was about me and was once again edging God out. The one thing that was most helpful was for me to quiet myself more often and remain open and alert to the Holy Spirit, no matter what I was doing. I learned that there are teachable moments happening all around you if you stop focusing on yourself." He smiled.

"Which brings me to what I think is the best advice I can give you: Get out and about. Learn as you listen. Ask the Holy Spirit to help you fall in love with God's people again. Then stand ready for an interesting journey. If you keep your heart available to God's love, be prepared to have it filled to overflowing.

"To guide you along the way," Hank continued, "I've thought about some people who can help you. In this envelope are the names of four people we both know, and I think each will have a special message to pass on to you. The name and a particular question for you to ask each person are on separate slips of paper so you can draw them out one at a time and in an order that only God knows."

"Sounds pretty mysterious," commented Tim. "But you have always seen a little farther and deeper into things than I have, so I guess I will follow your lead one more time. Thanks for being here for me when I needed a friend to talk to."

"My pleasure, Tim," said Hank.

Before Tim left, they bent their heads in prayer.

Driving home from his meeting with Hank, Tim felt both hopeful and excited that all was not lost. The first thing he did when he got home was to write down and review what he'd learned from Hank:

- A few minutes of brutal honesty are worth years of self-deception.

- God's love for me is bigger than any mistake or leadership miscue I can ever make.

- Having safe-harbor accountability relationships is a vital antidote to the pressures and isolation of leadership.

- Get out and about. Learn as you listen. Ask the Holy Spirit to help you fall in love with God's people again.

Chapter 5

A ROCKING CHAIR REVELATION

With Linda out of town, Tim had planned to devote Saturday
to some guilt-free sorting out of his tax records for the annual
"render unto Caesar" ordeal as well as watching the March
Madness basketball tournament.

Just as he was settling in, his daughter, Pam, called to ask a
big favor. She and her husband, Paul, were planning to attend
a wedding that afternoon. They had intended to leave baby
Hannah with Paul's mother, but she had just called to say that
she was exhibiting some early flu symptoms and would like to
renege on her offer to babysit. With the daughter-to-father
tone that always melted Tim, Pam asked if he would stand in

as the duty babysitter. After looking longingly at his tax project and the half-time score of a tight game, Tim said, "Sure. What time do you want me to come over?"

"How about fifteen minutes?" Pam replied. "We'll have everything all set up for you. The baby will probably sleep most of the time so it won't be too hard an assignment," she said with an optimistic tone.

"Great, sweetie pie. I'm sure we'll do just fine," Tim replied with more confidence than he was feeling at the moment.

When Tim arrived at Pam's house, however, things were not as advertised. Baby Hannah was wide awake, hungry, and in need of a change. The new mother and first-time father were running late, and Grandpa was asking himself what he had gotten into.

Despite his misgivings, Tim told the anxious couple to go on. He would handle the situation. He hadn't used his baby-sitting skills for quite a while but figured he could still change a diaper and handle a bottle feeding.

To Tim's relief, the diaper change went well, with both parties happy when it was over. He heated the bottle in a pan with some water in the bottom, and then he settled with baby and bottle into an old rocking chair that he and Linda had bought when their son, Andy, was born. Rocking back and forth in the quiet house drew Tim into a time of peaceful reflection he would never forget.

He remembered sitting in this same rocker when Andy

was just learning to walk. Andy would run toward him from across the room with his arms outstretched, a big smile on his face, full of confidence that his daddy would pick him up and give kisses that made him giggle even when he had a messy diaper.

Tim reflected on how unrestrained his little son had joyfully presumed and anticipated his love. He wondered whether he was accepting God's unconditional love in the same way.

Now, watching this little time traveler from the heart of God brought Tim a new sense of what it was to love and be loved unconditionally. Hannah wasn't striving at any great work. She wasn't trying to please him or anybody else. All she was doing was being what God, in His love, intended her to be—the object of His great, unconditional affection. Tim recalled that someone said that we were all made for God's pleasure. In that moment, in that old rocking chair, the Holy Spirit revealed to Tim that his granddaughter had been created for God's pleasure and for Tim's as well. He came into the presence of God's unconditional love in a new way through his love for a sleeping baby.

As Hannah fell asleep in his arms, Tim reflected on what he had learned from this touching moment:

♥ God has made us for His pleasure, and we are
   the objects of His great, unconditional love.

♥ Living with the unconditional love of God means surrendering your life to Him with the trust and joy of a child.

♥ God's unconditional love for us models how we may love one another.

Chapter 6

A BEDSIDE BLESSING

When he returned home from watching baby Hannah, Tim opened the envelope that Hank had given him. The first name he drew from the envelope—Clair Bowen, the director of women's ministries—was a surprise. She had come to Beacon Hill four years ago with a distinguished résumé as a Bible teacher. With quiet dignity, high intelligence, and a daunting work ethic, Clair had served the women of the church until her dormant cancer came out of remission some ten months ago. Since then, she had labored on between her aggressive treatments. Four weeks ago, Clair was admitted to the local hospital, and she was experiencing a slow but constant decline in her condition. Tim called the hospital and made arrangements to visit Clair after church on Sunday.

When he entered Clair's hospital room at the appointed time, she was propped up, holding the hands of a young woman in a hospital uniform. With eyes closed and head bowed, Clair prayed quietly as the young woman wept. When Clair finished praying, the two women exchanged an embrace, and the young hospital worker slipped quietly out of the room.

Clair greeted Tim with a warm and inviting smile. "Come in, Tim," she said. "How wonderful it is to see you! Thank you for coming. How are Linda and your new grandbaby, Hannah?"

"Both are well, thank you, Clair," replied Tim, marveling at her famous gift to recall names and special events in the lives of her acquaintances. "How are you feeling today?" he asked awkwardly.

"A little tired," Clair admitted, "but blessed. The Lord continues to provide me with the energy to do what He calls me to do today—even if it is just resting in a hospital bed and letting other people take care of me."

"From what I just observed, it seems that your bedside ministry is an active work of the kingdom," replied Tim with a smile.

"That's an encouraging thought, coming from the church chairman," stated Clair.

"If the only result of my visit was to encourage you and in

turn be blessed by seeing you and your young friend in prayer, it would have been well worth the trip," Tim responded.

"I heartily agree," said Clair, "but I sense another reason for your visit."

"There is, Clair," replied Tim. "Some things have happened recently that lead me to conclude that maybe the church leadership and I have let the love of God and God's people slip from its primary place in our church. It's my great desire to restore the love that's been lost before any more harm is done to the church. The reason I came to see you today is to seek your help by asking a specific question Hank Dalton suggested that really goes right to the heart of the issue I'm struggling with."

"Please ask," said Clair, "and I'll give the answer my best effort."

"My question is, How do you restore a love relationship with God that has grown cold?"

"I am honored to be asked. It's a blessing to think that God still may have some use for what I have learned from my mistakes and His victories," said Clair.

She paused a moment to reflect. "A couple of things come to mind that might help. I think the response you've gotten is right. I've felt more love in this hospital than I've felt in recent years at the church."

Tim winced. Hearing this kind of feedback again hurt.

"Let me ask you a question," continued Clair. "Why do you personally want to restore this lost love?

"In fact, if you're serious about this, I suggest you write down your answers. Take some time with them. It will be helpful to frame your answers in the form of a *so that* response. For example, finish the sentence 'I want to restore the lost love so that (blank), so that (blank), so that (blank), so that (blank), so that (blank), until you run out of reasons. Do not write down what you think the right answer should be. Just write down what comes to your mind in the order it comes," instructed Clair.

"While you're doing that, Tim, I'm going to rest my eyes for a few moments. It's been a long morning. If I happen to doze off, please wake me. I want to make the most of your visit," she said, laying her head on her pillow.

"Will do," replied Tim as he set about what he thought would be a two-minute exercise. Fifteen minutes later, Tim looked down with some astonishment at what he had written. It read:

I want to restore the lost love in the church . . .

so *that* God receives from me and everyone in the
church the honor and gratitude that He deserves,

so *that* I can stop feeling guilty about being a hypocrite
and a phony,

so *that* I can be counted as a grateful steward of His
grace and mercy,

so *that* I can be an authentic and trustworthy follower
and leader in His service,

so that my life and leadership will count for something
in God's eyes.

As he read his progressive responses, Tim became aware
of how many of his reasons for wanting to restore the lost love
in the church were centered on improving his self-image. It
was much more of a "give to get" set of reasons than he would
have hoped. He even toyed with the idea of replacing some of
his responses with something that sounded higher minded.
But having learned something about the value of brutal honesty with himself, Tim decided to share his answers with
Clair, warts and all.

Tim gently tapped Clair on her hand, and she awakened
from her brief sleep. "How did you do?" she asked.

"Not as nobly as I had anticipated," Tim acknowledged.
"In fact, given the level of self-interest my *so that*'s revealed, I
am embarrassed at what you will think of me when you hear
them, let alone what God must already think."

"Rest assured, Tim, this room is part of a no fault-no
judgment ward of the hospital. Your secret will be safe with
me and God," responded Clair with a smile.

With Clair's encouragement, Tim read his *so that* responses
out loud. They didn't sound any better than when he first wrote
them down.

"Well," said Clair, "that was an impressive bit of honest
self-assessment."

"Thanks for the compliment, Clair," said Tim, "but it sure doesn't paint a very pretty picture of my motives, even though the quest I am on seems right and good."

"Such things are rarely flattering to one's self-image," replied Clair, "but they do help clear away some of our self-constructed myths about how lovable we are and create an opportunity for greater understanding of the width and depth of God's grace and forgiveness. They also give you a true understanding of where you will be starting from when you seek to lead others. I think it is a true statement that you can't honestly ask others to serve a purpose higher than you have."

"I sure can see my need for His forgiveness, given the fact that I am more focused on my self-interest than on God and the people in our church," admitted Tim.

"Take heart," Clair encouraged him. "God is quick to respond with His grace to any movement toward Him and to refine it to His purposes. I learned this many years ago when I was on the mission field in a Third World country. I discovered by accident that I had been betrayed by a close friend and colleague in a very deep and personal way. I was afraid that if I revealed what had happened to the rest of our team, it would seriously damage our ability to carry out our calling. So I kept the offense to myself.

"My colleague never knew that I knew what she had done, nor did anyone else. As a result of my self-imposed isolation, I became increasingly cold and bitter toward my unknowing team members and toward God. I secretly blamed God for letting this happen to me and blamed my team members for not sensing my pain and coming to my rescue. As time passed, I became unloving and unlovely, even in my eyes.

"One day, while I was watching a woman forming bricks out of straw and cow dung to be used to build a new hut for her family, I had a new thought about my situation. It came to me that if I didn't do something constructive with the materials I had at hand, including my smelly hurt and anger, I would end up wasting my chance to be the good witness that I'd hoped to become.

"I also realized that I didn't have the spiritual energy that it would take to turn things around. In exhaustion, I remember crying out—no, more accurately, whispering—'Father, help me out of this cold pit I have dug for myself. I don't want to be here anymore. I want to love again. Help me let go of the hurt. Bring me back into the light of Your love.'

"To make a long story short," added Clair, "that was the starting point of my journey back. Through God's grace, I was able to come out of my isolation and, with a joyful spirit, reengage with my colleagues in doing the work we had been sent to do. All I had the strength to do was to turn my dirty face toward Him, and He kissed it."

As Clair finished her story and rested her head back on her pillow, a nurse came into the room and indicated that she would return in a few minutes to draw some blood. Tim sensed it was the right time to finish his visit.

"Thank you, Clair, for the gifts of your question and your story. They will make all the difference in the rest of my journey," Tim told her.

"Thank you for coming here and making this a very special day for me," replied Clair. "Before you go, Tim, there are two pieces of scripture that were particularly helpful to me when I was on my way back into the light. Would you read them to me and then let me offer a prayer on your behalf? The first is Psalm 51:10–12."

"It would be my honor," said Tim.

Taking Clair's Bible from the bed stand, he read, "Create in me a pure heart, O God, and renew a steadfast spirit within me. Do not cast me from your presence or take your Holy Spirit from me. Restore to me the joy of your salvation and grant me a willing spirit, to sustain me."

"As that passage suggests, we all fall short of perfection. But God promises us that His love is always with us. Turn to Romans 8:38–39."

Tim opened the Bible to the right page and read: "For I am convinced that neither death nor life, neither angels nor demons, neither the present nor the future, nor any powers, neither height nor depth, nor anything else in all creation, will be able to separate us from the love of God that is in Christ Jesus our Lord."

With a smile on her face, Clair said, "So, Tim, don't think

you have to invite God *back* into your life. He's always there, just waiting for you to acknowledge His presence and love." She reached out for Tim's hand and prayed, "Lord, bless Tim as he seeks the way back to raising You up as his first love. Teach him what he needs to know along the way, that he might be a bright and true beacon for others."

When they finished praying, Tim said good-bye and took the elevator down to the lobby. Before leaving the hospital, Tim reflected on the lessons he had learned from his time with Clair and recorded them in his notebook:

- Right causes do not guarantee right motives. Leaders who serve in God's name should check their motives to see if they truly glorify God or hide a deeper level of self-interest.

- Make sure that when you ask others to serve a higher purpose, you are honestly committed to that higher purpose as well.

- God meets acts of true repentance, no matter how feeble, with an outpouring of blessing through His transforming love.

- It is never too late to turn a wayward heart back to God.

Chapter 7

FORGIVEN MUCH, LOVE MORE

The second name Tim pulled from the envelope brought an instant smile to his face. Charlie Duck was one of his favorite people at Beacon Hill. As the longtime head of the maintenance and grounds crew, Charlie, an ex-navy submariner, was known for his glorious gardens, neat-as-a-pin appearance, and an ability to fix almost anything.

In the early days of his first term as church chairman, Tim had asked Charlie if it would be all right to follow him around on a typical workday. It was an idea Tim had used when he was a senior staff manager in a large manufacturing plant. Whenever Tim had felt he was becoming isolated from the realities of day-to-day operations, he arranged to shadow one of the frontline supervisors for a full work shift. In doing so, he was able to get a feel for what it was like to be on the receiving end of the communications and instructions that came down from the top of the hierarchy. Tim had always returned from those experiences impressed by the frontline people and their ingenuity in coping with the often competing demands of their jobs. His walk-around with Charlie Duck had impressed him the same way. Charlie's clear-eyed, plain-language assessment of the church and his genuine joy in the work he was doing were encouraging and comforting to a new church chairman.

Tim felt that in Charlie Duck he had someone to rely on to do good work and give him an honest assessment. Soon after their first walk-around, Tim dropped in on Charlie on a regular basis for a cup of Charlie's strong, navy-style coffee and an unofficial update on how things were going from Charlie's point of view.

It occurred to Tim that when he'd still been unsure of himself, he'd made regular visits with Charlie. Once he'd become more confident that he could handle the chairman job, he'd let his visits slide.

Tim looked down at the question that Hank had suggested he ask Charlie Duck:

How does God know you love Him?

What answer would I give? Tim wondered. He was still thinking about his answer that afternoon on his way to Charlie Duck's maintenance office. As he approached, Tim saw a note tacked to the door:

Tim—

Small emergency on the other side of the campus. Please make yourself comfortable. Try the coffee—it's as good as ever. I will be back in ten minutes.

Charlie

As Tim settled into the visitor's chair with a steaming cup of Charlie's famous, powerful midwatch coffee, a hand-carved sign mounted over a small mirror caught his attention. It read, "Forgiven Much, Love More." As Tim was pondering how the message of the sign played into his search, Charlie Duck entered the room.

"Hello, stranger," Charlie greeted Tim. "It's been quite a while since you've ventured belowdecks to check on the crew. Sorry to keep you waiting, but a furor was building in the seniors' Bible study due to a blinking fluorescent light that was impeding concentration on their review of the end times."

"No problem," said Tim with a smile. "I've been enjoying the surroundings and waiting for the first jolt to my nervous system from this diluted turpentine you lovingly call coffee."

"If I took offense at your unkind comments about my coffee," replied Charlie, "it would be an act of wounded pride that I would later have to confess, so I will instead forgive you and reap my proper reward." He smiled and poured his own cup of coal-black brew. "So what brings you here in the middle of a busy workweek?"

"A spiritual leadership issue has been brought to my attention," replied Tim, "and I could use your help in the form of an answer to a somewhat unusual question."

"I'd love to be of any help I can," said Charlie. "As long as it doesn't have to do with my understanding of how women think or why God made mosquitoes, I'll give it my best shot. Fire away."

"My question is this," said Tim. "How does God know you love Him?"

Charlie was silent a moment, with a thoughtful look on his face. "That is quite an unusual question," he observed. "We usually focus on the reverse question: How do we know God loves us?"

"I've been thinking all morning about how God knows I love Him, but everything I came up with sounded lame, inconsistent, or downright self-serving," said Tim.

"For example?" asked Charlie.

"My first thought was the time I spend alone with Him. Yet how often does that actually happen? The time I spend in prayer lately is pretty much limited to asking for help to survive the day or quickly fulfilling a promise I made to pray for someone in trouble."

Charlie nodded. "Know what you mean, my friend."

"Then I thought about the time I spend in Bible studies," Tim continued. "That's showing God I love Him, right? But I suddenly had this image of myself becoming impatient with the people who struggle and argue about points that are perfectly clear and convincing to me. I realized I was turning it into a research project rather than taking nourishment from His Word. I'm not sure God really feels loved by me during those times."

"Okay, so you have a couple of areas to work on," said Charlie.

"No, there's more. Much more. I thought about my commitment to trust in Him and 'lean not on my own understanding' when problems come my way. But more often than not I assume control without consulting Him. Rather than take that time with God, I come up with quick-fix answers to protect my time and agenda from interruptions.

"I tried to congratulate myself for regularly attending worship services. But have I been showing God I love Him in church? Honestly, no. My mind is usually on how other people are responding to the new music format or the quality of the pastor's message."

"Sounds like you're just trying to be sure that your church members have a good experience," Charlie offered.

"Yeah, but if I search my heart, it's more about having control than loving the people whom I supposedly serve in God's name. The truth is, I still have unresolved anger toward some of the people who engineered the unwarranted firing of the former pastor."

Tim sighed. "All my answers to the question of how God knows I love Him—praying, reading the Bible, going to worship services, tithing, and treating people right—sounded like a spiritual maintenance checklist. Something is definitely missing."

"When those to-dos are done with the right spirit and for the right reasons, they are part of showing God that we love Him," said Charlie. He pointed at the sign that Tim had read earlier: Forgiven Much, Love More. "Just keep that in mind, and you'll do all right," he said.

"What does it mean exactly?" Tim asked.

"It reminds me what Jesus did for me and what Jesus is calling me to do. Wherever you see yourself falling short, remember that you're forgiven. Keep your focus on His command to love."

Tim thought about the letter he'd received: *Accept the challenge to restore love into the life of the church by reviving the passion and humility that were present when the church was first starting out.*

"How do you show God you love Him?" Tim asked.

"Two ways," replied Charlie. "One is by admitting I'm broken and letting Him do the fixing."

"Coming from the world's greatest fix-it man, that sounds

pretty remarkable," Tim commented. "What do you mean by admitting you're broken?"

"To me, it means being vulnerable and willing to take my faults, fears, and failures to God. It means giving Him the glory for anything I might get prideful about."

"And what do you mean by letting Him do the fixing?" Tim asked.

"That means surrendering control to God. Once we're willing, He's the One who can fix a prideful and fearful heart and make it ready for service. My part of the fixing process is staying on ready alert to obey His commands. That means having a loving heart and making loving choices for love of the One who has forgiven me much and loves me even more."

"What's the second way you show God you love Him?" asked Tim.

"Father's Day cards," replied Charlie.

"You've got to be kidding," said Tim in astonishment.

"Never been more serious in my life," responded Charlie. "Let me explain. I had a pretty rough start when I was growing up. My dad was an alcoholic who used to take out his frustrations by beating on me and my little brother. As soon as I could, I left home and joined the navy to get as far away from him as possible. It wasn't until an old chief bosun's mate named Hayden Fry introduced me to my heavenly Father that the term *father* had anything but bad memories for me. Even then, it took me quite a while to trust in the fact that I had been accepted into

His family as a beloved child. Once I finally got it, I tried to live each day as a thank-you to my heavenly Father.

"That's where the idea that 'every day is Father's Day' for Charlie Duck comes from. From the time I get up until the time I go to bed, I stay alert for things to admire that He has prepared for me to see and do. Throughout the day, I'm working on that day's Father's Day card. Before I get into bed, I thank Him for a day that will never come again. Before I go to sleep at night, I thank Him for all the good things that have happened during the day and ask Him to help me accept and learn from the bad.

"That's about as plain and simple as I can make it," concluded Charlie. "I hope that helps, Tim."

Before Tim could answer, the phone on Charlie's desk rang. Charlie picked it up and, after listening for a few seconds, said, "May I suggest you take a five-minute break? I'll be right over."

"What's up?" Tim asked as Charlie hung up the phone.

"I'm sorry to have to cut our visit short, Tim, but the end times seem to have arrived ahead of schedule at the seniors' Bible study. The overhead projector has blown a fuse."

"No problem," Tim said with a laugh. "You've given me lots to think about."

After Charlie left the office, Tim took a final sip of his coffee and opened his notebook to record the wisdom he'd gleaned during their meeting:

♥ Remember: Forgiven Much, Love More.

♥ Admit you're broken and let God do the fixing.

♥ Stay alert and ready to obey commands with a loving heart, through loving choices, for the love of the One who loved you first.

♥ Live as if every day is Father's Day for those who love the Lord.

Chapter 8

A ROADBLOCK TO LOVE

If Charlie Duck's name brought joy to Tim's heart, the next name he drew from the envelope was one that instantly filled him with dread: Gordon Phillips.

At one time, Gordon had been one of Tim's closest friends at Beacon Hill. Both men had joined the church about the same time and started to serve in church leadership about the same time as well. Their families had enjoyed many happy times together at Family Camp and working alongside one another in putting on the annual all-church picnic. Beverly Phillips and Tim's wife, Linda, had been close confidantes and the mainstays of the Baby Bouncing Corps in the nursery at the first service. But everything changed during the furor over the firing of the former pastor.

As the outgoing church chairman during those tumultuous times, Gordy had been the main proponent of dismissing the pastor. Tim fought long and passionately for the pastor's retention. The weeks of emergency meetings and heated debate strained their relationship to the breaking point. When, by the slimmest of margins, the vote at the church council went in favor of dismissal, Tim felt alienated and angry. He focused many of his negative feelings on Gordy because Tim felt Gordy abused his power as chairman by ruling to limit debate and force a final vote.

Although they had continued to serve together until the end of Gordy's term and departure from the council, their relationship had never recovered. Both remained in the church, yet Tim and Gordon managed—as though by an unspoken agreement—to steer clear of each other.

Now, Hank was asking Tim to swallow his pride and seek out his old nemesis. The question he was to ask Gordy just added to Tim's unsettled state of mind. It read:

As brothers in Christ, what do we owe each other?

Tim knew the answer. Jesus said it plainly in His timeless command: "As I have loved you, so you must love one another" (John 13:34).

But how? Tim wondered. He suddenly recalled the description of love that Hank had quoted from 1 Corinthians 13:

love keeps no record of wrongs, is not easily angered, is not proud, is hopeful, and is kind.

Deep in his heart, Tim knew that as brothers in Christ, he and Gordy Phillips owed that love to each other. And hadn't Jesus said something about forgiving his brother not seven times, but seventy times seven?

It sounded good—in theory. But as he thought about forgiving Gordy, something inside Tim resisted. At the center of what he was feeling was unresolved anger toward Gordy that he had buried way down inside. On top of that was the tremendous guilt he felt for not being able to forgive Gordy. Hank's question had thrown up a major roadblock to Tim's ability to love, and now he couldn't get past it. He was stuck.

How was he going to spearhead a return to God's love for Beacon Hill Community Church when he himself couldn't express it? It was with a lonely and discouraged spirit that Tim entered the weekend.

On Sunday morning as he always did, Tim joined the other elders at the front of the worship center to pray with any folks who needed prayer. On this Sunday, no one approached Tim for prayer. In a way he was relieved, given the unsettled state of his spirit. But just as he was about to head home, a shy teenage girl with a smile full of braces approached Tim and asked him to pray for her about the next week at school.

Despite his gloomy mood, Tim obliged in a very loving

prayer. When he thought that their time together was over, the girl looked up at Tim and asked, "Can I pray for you?"

He was stunned by the question. The sweetness in her face melted him inside. "Yes," Tim said softly, "I would like that very much."

"What is it that I can pray for?" she asked.

"Well," replied Tim, "I've been looking for something that I've lost and I'm having trouble finding it. I could sure use some prayer to help me get unstuck."

"Sure," said the teenager. As they bowed their heads together, she spoke to God in the most natural and familiar way: "Please, God, help Mr. Tim find what he is looking for. He looks like he has a lot on his mind and could really use Your help. In Jesus' name, amen!"

Holding back his tears, Tim thanked the girl for her prayer.

"Anytime," she replied with a smile. "I'll be praying for you this week. Bye!"

As Tim watched her run back up the aisle, he realized he'd found some of what he had been searching for: God's love poured out through His people. At that moment he knew that the way back to love was to open his heart to the healing power of the community. It wasn't going to be easy to resolve his relationship with Gordy Phillips, but it was going to be a lot easier now, knowing that someone was praying for him.

When he got into his car, he picked up the journal he'd

left on the seat and put into words what he'd relearned that
weekend:

- ♥ As sisters and brothers in Christ, we owe one
  another what Jesus said plainly in His timeless
  command: "As I have loved you, so you must love
  one another."

- ♥ The love of God comes to each of us through
  His Word and through His people.

- ♥ Forgiveness is love in action.

Chapter 9

REACHING OUT

Now that her mother was fully recovered, Linda was returning that afternoon. As he drove to the airport to pick her up, Tim tried to figure out how to make peace with Gordy Phillips. He knew that at this point, even if he got up the nerve to call him, it would be a hollow gesture to fulfill his promise to Hank. First he needed to come to terms with his unresolved pride and anger. Tim knew he should forgive Gordy, but he also knew in his heart of hearts that it was something only God could make happen.

He thought back on his visits with Hank, Clair, and Charlie, replaying in his mind what had been revealed to him about himself. He recalled when Hank helped him see that his pride was hurt by the thought that the church had walked away from God as its first love on his watch. He remembered how self-centered most of his reasons for seeking to return God to first-love status seemed when he answered Clair's *so that* question. He reflected on the "Forgiven Much, Love More" sign in Charlie's office.

As he again felt the weight of the burden he was carrying inside, the traffic ahead on the freeway began to thicken and finally came to a stop. Tim could see the flashing lights of emergency vehicles and highway patrol cars ahead around the scene of a recent accident.

Just what I need, Tim thought. *Now I'm stuck two ways. Stuck in traffic and stuck in trying to figure out what to do next with Gordy Phillips.*

As the traffic inched forward, Tim sensed that he was being moved closer and closer to the answers to his soul-searing questions—even if it was only a few inches at a time. The sweet encouragement from his young prayer partner and his rocking-chair reconnection with unconditional love seemed to be much more than random events along the way.

Tim knew he must discover the answers to these questions before he could tackle the task of leading the church back to a place where love came first. Something was missing that Tim couldn't quite put his finger on.

Suddenly he experienced a blinding flash of the obvious. *Why am I trying to figure this out on my own?* he thought. Then he remembered Charlie Duck's words about admitting you're broken and letting God do the fixing. Up until now, he still had been trying to fix things by himself and not letting God take the lead.

He couldn't bow his head because he needed to keep his eyes on the road, but Tim prayed out loud in the silence of his car: "Father God, forgive me for edging You out and trying to figure things out on my own. Lord, I want to serve You and not my own ego. Help me, Father, to have a heart that listens and responds to Your love and guidance. Help me see things through Your eyes and have the courage to think and act out of love, not out of pride and fear.

"Father, I'm putting down my anger and hurt feelings toward Gordy Phillips, along with my pride and my fears, at the foot of the cross. Help me not to pick them up again. In Jesus' name, amen."

As he finished praying, Tim felt a great weight lift from his heart. He didn't know what would happen when he called Gordy, but whatever happened, he knew he wouldn't have to face it alone. With newfound peace, Tim picked up his cell phone and asked information for the number of Gordon Phillips.

When he was connected to Gordon's voice mail and prompted to leave a message, Tim responded, "Hi, Gordy, this is Tim Manning. Sorry I missed you. Look, I was wondering if we could get together for coffee in the next couple of days. If you're willing, I'd like to see if we can clear the air on some unfinished business we've had between us. Please give me a call. Thanks."

Two days after leaving his phone message, Tim received an unexpected response from Gordy Phillips in the form of an e-mail message. It read:

Tim,

I was surprised to receive your call the other day. After giving it much thought, I have decided to decline your invitation to meet. If there is any unfinished business between us, it is old business, and I am not inclined to open up old wounds for the sake of clearing the air. Better let sleeping dogs lie.

Sincerely,

Gordy

As he stared at his computer screen, Tim was stunned by how his attempt at extending forgiveness and reconciliation had been rejected completely. In his mind's eye, Tim had imagined offering a gift of forgiveness and an apology to Gordy and receiving acceptance and reconciliation in return. What he'd received instead was cold rejection.

Tim's initial reactions were anger and sadness. He was angry at Gordy Phillips for his lack of interest in even trying to reconcile their differences. That, in turn, rekindled some of the old, unresolved feelings toward Gordy he had felt during the heat of their dispute over the firing of the pastor. Tim was sad because he thought that unless he could overcome his unloving feelings toward Gordy, he was never going to complete his quest of restoring God to first-love status in his life—and in the church. Perhaps he was putting too much importance on restoring this relationship, but that's how he felt.

When Tim shared what had happened with Linda, he was in for another surprise. Instead of letting him convene a pity party, she challenged him with one of her classic thought-provoking questions.

"If you really want to get past this situation with Gordy, what choices do you have about how to respond to what just happened?" she inquired.

"Not many," replied Tim. "In fact, probably only one—to get my ego out of the way. It's going to be hard, but I need to forgive Gordy again because I love God enough to be obedient to His Word."

"What can you do right now to make that happen?" asked Linda.

Tim thought a moment. "I know I can't do it on my own," he said. "The temptation to hold on to hurt feelings and bitterness is too strong. What I need to do is pray and turn it over to God. Let Him handle it."

"When is the best time to do that?" responded Linda.

"The sooner, the better," Tim replied with a knowing smile.

"As you have told me a hundred times before, it shows God I love Him when I make prayer my first response instead of my last resort."

"I am always glad to discover that what I say actually does make it into your memory bank," replied Linda with a smile.

"I'm glad you're glad," said Tim. "Honey, would you pray with me? I could use your support."

"Of course," Linda agreed.

As Tim and Linda sat holding hands with their heads bowed, Tim admitted to God that he wanted to remain angry and unforgiving toward Gordy Phillips. "I know You have called me to forgive and love him," said Tim. "As hard as I may try on my own, I know it will take the work of the Holy Spirit to change my heart."

Tim surrendered to God his anger and hurt feelings toward Gordy Phillips and asked that his relationship with Gordy be healed. Finally he prayed for Gordy: "Melt his heart and make him open to new levels of peace and harmony in his life."

Linda then offered her own prayer: "Heavenly Father, Tim and Gordy have wounded each other in their passion to do what they thought was right. Father, in Your time and in Your way, pour Your grace and mercy into their relationship so they may be reconciled. Father, I also want to surrender my resentment of how this rift between Tim and Gordy has caused my relationship with Bev Phillips to grow cold. I have missed her friendship and feel sad whenever our paths cross. Create in me a clean heart, Lord, and renew a right spirit in me as well. In Jesus' name, amen."

After sitting in silence for a minute, Tim said with a tone of regret, "Linda, I am so sorry. I can't believe it. But until just a moment ago, I never focused any attention on how my disagreements with Gordy had affected you and your relationship with Bev. If I had realized that it was not all about me and my injured pride, maybe things could have been different. Maybe if I had been quicker to ask for help to forgive and sought reconciliation earlier, Gordy and I could have extended each other some grace and put these issues behind us. I truly apologize for the heartache I have caused you and ask for your forgiveness."

"You already have it," replied Linda.

Later that evening before going upstairs to bed, Tim sat at the kitchen table with his journal and tried to piece together all he had learned since drawing Gordy Phillips's name from the envelope. He wrote:

- True grace and true forgiveness do not depend on the response they receive.

- Loving and forgiving us were risks that Jesus was willing to take.

- Just as they suffer from inhaling secondhand smoke, innocent people can pay a dear price for an unforgiving spirit.

♥ We show our love for God when we forgive others.

♥ God freely gives us the power to love and forgive if we ask for it.

Chapter 10

FINDING SELF-WORTH

As Tim looked at the name on the last slip of paper in the envelope and the question he was to ask, he knew that this might be the most challenging part of his journey to date. The name he read was his own. The question was:

Have you forgiven yourself?

He knew that if he were to take on the challenges to love and forgive that lay ahead, he had to let go of the temptation to keep beating himself up over the past. But despite the fact that he had been reassured of God's unconditional love, had asked God for His forgiveness, and had faith that he had received it, Tim realized his answer to the question had to be no.

Tim spent a troubled morning grappling with the question. Then it occurred to him to ask for help on this important question.

Fortunately he had a great counselor right under his own roof.

"Usually I don't have any trouble forgiving myself," he said to Linda after telling her about the latest question. "In fact, sometimes I might be a little too quick to cut myself some slack."

"No comment," Linda said with a knowing smile.

"A lot of the time I'll chalk up my miscues and the little messes I create to being human. But what's going on at Beacon Hill is different. I feel so responsible for letting people down—people who were looking to me for leadership."

"Seems to me you've put in a lot of hard work for the church," Linda observed. "And I know your intentions have been good."

Tim waved a dismissive hand. "You know what they say about good intentions. The fact is, I've grieved God, and my failures have had a negative impact on a whole congregation."

"Don't you think you're being a little too hard on yourself?" his wife said. "I doubt you'd be this tough on anyone else."

"It's easier to forgive other people because it's a one-way process. The only decision I have to make is to be willing to give forgiveness, and then my part is done. But to forgive myself, I have to be willing to give forgiveness and accept it as well."

"Are you unwilling to give forgiveness or accept it or both?" asked Linda.

"Probably both," replied Tim.

"So what's holding you back?" Linda probed.

Even as she asked the question, Tim had an inkling that he knew the answer, but he wasn't yet willing to admit it. Silently he asked the Holy Spirit to reveal the source of his reluctance. When the answer came, Tim was startled by its clarity. Feeling embarrassed, he looked down at the floor.

Linda studied his troubled expression. "What is it?" she said.

"I'm almost ashamed to say," he replied.

She said, "I'm your wife. You can tell me."

"I'm beginning to realize that my inadequate performance has inflicted wounds on my self-image. I'm worried about what others will think of me. That's what's holding me back from forgiving myself."

Linda put her hand on his arm and gave it a squeeze. "I love you when you tell the truth," she said. "Welcome to the human race. I'm reminded of a book by Robert S. McGee I read years ago called *The Search for Significance*. He wrote that if there was a formula for self-worth Satan would love you to buy into, it's that your self-worth is the sum total of your performance and the opinion of others."

"That's brilliant," said Tim. "And so true!"

"To have your self-esteem up for grabs every day based on how well you perform or what other people think of you is to live an always anxious, always at-risk, never secure, never satisfied life. High sensitivity to negative feedback is a sure symptom of this kind of self-centered thinking. Any indications that your performance is inadequate or your reputation is at risk quickly become a threat to the safety of your self-esteem, to be resisted or denied."

"That sure applies to this situation," said Tim. "I've edged out God and His love and forgiveness. What's taken God's place is my performance-based opinion of myself. It's interesting. While God is merciful and forgiving, my pride sure isn't! It seems that if I forgive myself, my pride will lose its right to punish me for the damage it's suffered. And it's not finished beating me up yet!"

"I suggest you start praying to get that monkey off your back," said Linda.

Tim nodded. "I'm going to do that now," he said. He went out to the yard and sat in his favorite spot beneath a massive old cypress tree. With his back leaning against the tree trunk, he called out to God in prayer, confessing that he'd been worried more about his bruised ego and reputation than about the church. He asked God for the wherewithal to deal with the consequences of the past in a right and loving way.

Tim kept his eyes closed, listening to the sounds of the

birds chirping and the breeze rustling through the leaves overhead. He felt a sense of peace about the trials that were to come. He now felt confident that his self-worth was secure in the love and forgiveness of Jesus Christ, and was no longer up for grabs based on his performance and the opinion of others.

Tim knew he was being called to be an active agent of love-based leadership. Keeping this kind of leadership foremost in his mind, Tim prepared for the next step on the journey to restore love to the church: going public with the letter he had received. His first contact would be Pastor Mike on his return from sabbatical.

As he walked back into the house, he mentally reviewed what he'd learned so far that day:

♥ Get your ego out of the way, and ask for help when you need it.

♥ Give yourself some slack—leave room for God's grace.

♥ Recognize that forgiveness starts with yourself.

Chapter 11

BUILDING HIS CHURCH

Pastor Mike Reston and his wife, Jane, watched the shuttle driver load their luggage into the van. They were leaving the lakeside cottage of Jane's mom and dad, where they'd had the privilege of spending a two-month sabbatical.

"I'm sure glad I married you, honey—particularly since you came with your parents' cottage," said Mike jokingly.

Jane laughed. "It has been wonderful, hasn't it? To tell you the truth, I'm a little reluctant to leave."

"Why's that?"

Jane sighed. "It's been so nice having you around every day and not being on call twenty-four/seven to the needs of the ministry."

"I know what you mean," Mike stated as he opened the

back door of the van. He slid into the backseat beside her and said, "Another thing I've really appreciated about this sabbatical is that it's given me some time to think—to look at the ministry and see my role more clearly."

Jane took a moment to give their flight information to the driver before turning back to Mike. "Of all the things you've learned that we've talked about this summer, what were your biggest *ahas?*" she asked.

Mike gave it some thought. "For one thing," he said, "I'm more sure than ever that my primary calling is to preach and inspire the spiritual growth of the congregation. That said, I'm also clear that I was incredibly worn out and really needed this break."

"Worn out by what?" asked Jane.

"You've already nailed it. Trying to keep track twenty-four/seven of all the things that are going on and working to make sure they're successful."

"And who is at least partly responsible for that?" asked Jane with a smile.

Mike looked over at his wife. "Me," he admitted.

That was one thing Pastor Mike loved most about Jane— her commitment to supporting his best self. "I guess I've been trying to be Superman again," he said.

Jane nodded. "And how many years have you been working on that?" she asked.

"Quite a few," he replied. "I still remember our first conversation on this topic back in graduate school. After a few dates you said, 'Reston, I think you're all right, but you seem to have a Superman complex. You think you have to figure everything out by yourself.' You told me you thought I was good, but not that good!"

Jane laughed, and Mike smiled at the memory. She'd been right, of course. Not to mention refreshingly direct. No one had ever talked to him like that before, much less a girl he was just getting to know.

"In fairness to you," said Jane, "there is an awful lot going on at Beacon Hill. People have come to count on you to leap tall buildings—or at least get them funded."

Mike and Jane rode in thoughtful silence as the shuttle van made its way to the airport. After a time, Mike said, "Another thing that became clear to me over the past several weeks is that I haven't felt joyful about my ministry at Beacon Hill for a long time."

"Honey, knowing you the way I do, that's always been a warning sign that something is headed in the wrong direction," said Jane. "Tell me more."

"I've had a gnawing feeling that despite the fact that the ministry is growing, we may be losing a very basic part of what made ministry so exciting when we first came to Beacon Hill. Something has been happening that's in conflict with what the church is supposed to be. So I went back to the Gospels to see exactly what Jesus said about the church."

"Really? This is news to me," said Jane. "What did you find out?"

"The first time Jesus mentioned the church was in Matthew 16:18, when He said, 'I will build my church, and the gates of Hades will not overcome it.'"

"It sounds like Jesus was very clear about what He had in mind for something that didn't exist yet," said Jane.

"That's exactly what I thought," replied Mike. "Jesus claimed full ownership of the church as well as retaining full responsibility for building it. Remember He said, '*I* will build *my* church . . .' The church was something very personal and very special to Him. This whole train of thought led me to study the word *church*, which reaffirmed what I learned during my divinity school days—that when Jesus said, 'I will build my church,' He was talking about more than a building or organizational structure. He was talking about creating a living, breathing community of people."

"Going by that definition, how would you say Beacon Hill is stacking up?" asked Jane.

"By that definition, not so great," said Mike. "I think we were evaluating the health of Beacon Hill by the size and condition of buildings, the numbers and models of cars in our parking lot, the quality and style of our music, the number of weekend services, the weekday programs, and attendance at the Christmas and Easter pageants. But these are all external measures that were giving me a false, positive impression of the health of our church. What I've learned is that what really matters is what's going on in the relationships inside Beacon Hill. That, I realize, is where we need some work."

"You have been doing a lot of thinking about this," noted Jane.

"I have," said Mike. He reached into his carry-on bag and pulled out a sheaf of papers. "I took the time to write out seven characteristics that define the church Jesus had in mind:

"First, *love was to be the distinct internal characteristic* that guided the lives and relationships of the church community. In John 13:34–35 Jesus said, 'A new command I give you: Love one another. As I have loved you, so you must love one another. By this all men will know that you are my disciples, if you love one another.'

"Second, *His church would be an everlasting community* of interdependent people called in time and circumstance to glorify God. The church would be unified by love: on the inside, love among members; on the outside, making the love of Jesus known to the world.

"Third, *His church would have all the resources it required* to fulfill its mission. In Matthew 28:18–20 Jesus said, 'All authority in heaven and on earth has been given to me. Therefore go and make disciples of all nations, baptizing them in the name of the Father and of the Son and of the Holy Spirit, and teaching them to obey everything I have commanded you. And surely I am with you always, to the very end of the age.'

"Fourth, *His church would have prayer as the most distinctive practice* of its daily life and relationship with Him. In Matthew 21:13 Jesus said, 'My house will be called a house of prayer.'

"Fifth, *His church would have ongoing access to an unimpeachable source of knowledge, wisdom, and power* to guide its actions. In John 14:26 Jesus said, 'The Holy Spirit, whom the Father will send in my name, will teach you all things and will remind you of everything I have said to you.' And He promised in Acts 1:8: 'You will receive power when the Holy Spirit comes on you; and you will be my witnesses in Jerusalem, and in all Judea and Samaria, and to the ends of the earth.'

"Sixth, *His church would have His guidance.* Jesus promised to always remain actively involved in the work-in-progress of His church in and through the lives and relationships of His people. In Matthew 18:20 He said, 'For where two or three come together in my name, there am I with them.'

"When Jesus spoke of building His church, He evoked the sense of an ongoing process that will reach completion only on His terms and in His time," said Mike.

"Seventh, *He would sustain the church.* Actively seeking and submitting to the direction and design criteria that Jesus had established for His church would determine whether any value was being added by the human efforts done in His name. In John 15:5 Jesus said, 'I am the vine; you are the branches. If a man remains in me and I in him, he will bear much fruit; apart from me you can do nothing.'"

Mike put down his papers and turned to Jane. "Any thoughts?" he asked.

"Yes. I think you've used your sabbatical time well," said Jane. "I see some retooling in Beacon Hill's future."

"I agree," said Mike. "And we'll be focused on three things." He summed them up for Jane as follows:

- Love of God's people for one another remains the defining characteristic of Jesus' church.

- Love continues to be the foundation of His church's impact and reputation in the world.

- Jesus is still actively at work refining His church, using imperfect people and leaders who are willing to surrender their weaknesses, pride, and fear to the guidance of the Holy Spirit.

Chapter 12

A CHANCE ENCOUNTER?

Pastor Mike Reston was deep in thought as he stared out the airplane window onto the sea of clouds that stretched to the horizon. Across the aisle, Jane was enjoying one of her favorite activities, working her way through a crossword puzzle.

As he looked at the patchwork of farmland that occasionally appeared through breaks in the cloud layer below, Mike reviewed what had become clear to him about himself and his ministry at Beacon Hill. He had reaffirmed that his primary calling was to preach and inspire the spiritual growth of his congregation.

After his conversation with Jane, he had also come to grips with the fact that something was missing in the life of the church. Beacon Hill wasn't quite the heaven on earth he dreamed it could be, and it certainly wasn't the purposeful community that Jesus had envisioned. Mike couldn't put his finger on why. He knew his heart was in the right place, yet he also had to admit that trying to live up to the image of a twenty-four/seven pastor had drained the joy from his work. He was frankly weary of the always churning relationships that made up the life of the church. Over the past year or two, the endless petty rivalries had caused him to slowly withdraw his emotional investment in leading Beacon Hill.

He bowed his head and silently prayed: *Lord, show me how to be the leader You have in mind.*

"Sir, would you care for anything to drink?" The flight attendant smiled down at him, interrupting his prayer.

"Just water, thanks," he replied.

The flight attendant gave him his water and took the order of the passenger sitting next to him.

The plane jolted, hitting a pocket of turbulence, and the ice in his cup shifted. Mike's thoughts turned to the likely challenges ahead: contested budgets, squabbles over meeting spaces, a way to finance long overdue repairs, interpersonal differences and competition, and the usual criticisms of his sermons. Mike exhaled heavily, letting out an unintentional groan.

"My goodness," said the passenger sitting next to him, looking up from his book. "That's quite a heavy sigh."

Mike turned to the passenger, an affable-looking fellow

wearing glasses and a big grin. Looking into the man's smiling face, Mike got the strange feeling he'd seen him somewhere before.

"Sounds like you've got the weight of the world on your shoulders," the passenger said.

Mike laughed. "Yeah, my wife over here calls it my Superman complex."

From across the aisle, Jane looked up with a smile.

"I guess I was thinking through some work-related leadership issues and reacted to my thoughts a little too loudly," said Mike to the passenger beside him. "Sorry to interrupt your reading."

"What kind of business are you in?" the passenger asked.

"I'm a church pastor. My name's Mike Reston."

"Hello, Mike," said the passenger, extending his hand. "I'm Vince Blakely."

That name rang a bell, along with his face. "Do I know you from somewhere?" Mike asked.

"Maybe," Vince said with a shrug. "I've written a couple of books. My expertise is business management and leadership."

Mike marveled at how God worked. Here he asked God to help him be the kind of leader He wanted, and suddenly an expert appeared next to him.

"You're lucky," Vince said. "When it comes to leadership, you church pastors have a real competitive edge. You have the greatest role model of all time."

"Really?" said Mike. "Who's that?"

"Why, Jesus of Nazareth, of course!"

For a moment Mike thought the author was mocking him.

"Seriously," Vince continued, "I'd been studying leadership for years. So when I turned over my life to the Lord in my late forties and started to read about Jesus and what He did with those twelve unlikely followers in just three years, I was blown away. Everything I'd ever learned about great leadership, Jesus did. And He did it perfectly."

Mike shook his head in wonder. "That's amazing because I was just praying to the Lord to show me the kind of leader He wanted me to be. But I didn't realize until now that His answer would be, 'Follow Me.'"

"Why is that so surprising to you?" asked Vince.

"I've always thought of Jesus as my Lord and Savior, but I never thought of Him as a teacher of leadership. I feel a teachable moment here. Do you mind if I pick your brain a bit?"

"Not at all," said Vince.

Mike pulled out a sheet of paper to capture the gems he had a feeling were to come. "Tell me what you've learned about Jesus as a leader."

"First," explained Vince, "I believe it's always a good practice to define your terms. So let me give you my definition of *leadership*. I believe that leadership is an influence process. Anytime you're engaged in influencing the thinking, behavior, or development of others, you're engaged in leadership.

"Leadership is not just about positions. There's organizational leadership—CEOs, presidents, and the like—and life-role leadership—moms, dads, teachers, coaches, and the like."

Mike nodded his head in agreement. "So that means Jesus can be a leadership role model at home and in the community as well as at work."

"That's right," said Vince. "And like every great leader, Jesus had a defined leadership point of view. Where He stated it most clearly was in the book of Matthew."

Mike nodded. "I know where you're going with this. It's in Matthew 20:25–28." He quoted the verses: "Jesus called them together and said, 'You know that the rulers of the Gentiles lord it over them, and their high officials exercise authority over them. Not so with you. Instead, whoever wants to become great among you must be your servant, and whoever wants to be first must be your slave—just as the Son of Man did not come to be served, but to serve, and to give his life as a ransom for many.'"

"You really are a pastor, aren't you?" said Vince. "What really interested me about that statement was that Jesus was calling His disciples to be servant leaders. And this wasn't a suggestion—it was a mandate."

"*Servant leadership* is a term I've heard about a lot," Mike said, "but to be honest, I haven't seen it much in action."

"That's because like so many things in life, servant leadership is a lot easier to say than to do," noted Vince. "In my past work in leadership, I focused mainly on the head—people's

beliefs about leading and motivating people—and the hands—
how they put those beliefs into action. It wasn't until I turned
my life over to the Lord that I realized there are two other
dimensions that are probably even more important—the heart
and habits of a leader."

"Why is the heart so important in leadership?" Mike
asked.

"Effective servant leadership is an inside job. It's about character and intention. Are you leading to serve or to be served?
You've got to answer that question honestly. You can't fake being
a servant leader because when problems crop up—as they inev-
itably do—people who have a self-serving leader will pull away
instead of pull together."

Mike cringed inside, thinking over his laundry list of problems related to Beacon Hill and his desire to pull away. "Suppose
I have a friend who's leading a church that seems to be pulling
apart instead of pulling together. What advice would you give
my friend?" he asked.

Vince smiled. "I would tell your *friend*"—he drew out the
word with a wink—"that his leadership starts with the heart.
If his heart is motivated by self-interest, he's in trouble. In other
words, is he putting his agenda, safety, status, and gratification
ahead of those who are affected by his leadership decisions? Or
is he really thinking about what's best for others?"

"I'm sure he'd say he's motivated by his heart, but how can
he really know?" Mike asked.

"Two ways," Vince replied. "The first is how he receives criticism. Have you ever tried to give feedback to someone up the hierarchy, and that person killed the messenger? If you've ever experienced that, you were dealing with a self-serving leader. These kinds of leaders hate feedback."

Mike recalled the brouhaha about last year's Easter pageant. His not wanting to hear more about it was partly behind what motivated him to go on sabbatical. He felt his cheeks flush with shame.

"It's not that self-serving leaders are always arrogant," continued Vince. "It's often insecurity. If you give them a negative assessment, they think you don't want them to lead anymore. And that's their worst nightmare because they identify so strongly with their position. They forget they're just human, like everyone else."

"So how does a servant leader handle feedback?" asked Mike.

"Real servant leaders love to hear what others think," Vince replied. "They know the only reason they're leading is to serve, and if anybody has any suggestions on how they can serve better, they want to hear them. They consider feedback—even when it comes in the form of criticism—a gift. When they receive a critique, their first response is, 'Thank you. That's really helpful. Can you tell me more? Is there anybody else I should talk to?'"

"This is really helpful," said Mike. "I have to admit that

sometimes I resist feedback. But in my defense, sometimes I am overwhelmed with all my responsibilities."

"I realize that," said Vince, "but that could be your fault. You see, the second giveaway of self-serving leaders is their unwillingness to develop other leaders around them. They fear the potential competition for their leadership position."

In that moment Mike knew that Vince had been heaven-sent. For weeks he'd wanted to ask for help from Tim Manning, the chairman of the Elder Council. He had to admit that fear had held him back.

"This is really helpful. Can you tell me more?" said Mike with a smile.

"Absolutely," Vince said warmly. "Another trait of servant leaders is that they think leadership is not the province of just the formal leaders. To them, leadership should emerge everywhere. They want to bring out the best in others. If a good leader rises, servant leaders are willing to partner with that person, and even step aside and take a different role if necessary. They thrive on developing others, and they encourage individuals with expertise to come forward as needed. The scholar of servant leadership, Robert Greenleaf, said that the true test of a servant leader is this: Do those around the servant leader become wiser, freer, more autonomous, healthier, and better able to become servant leaders?"

Mike let out a big sigh as he took in all of Vince's comments.

"You mentioned a fourth dimension of servant leadership, habits. Tell me a little bit about that."

"This was the most surprising to me as I examined the leadership of Jesus," said Vince. "The reality is that there are all kinds of pressures and temptations on us every day to get off track and become self-serving rather than serving leaders. Jesus modeled incredible consistency in His daily habits of solitude, prayer, and application of Scripture. My favorite story about His habits is in Mark 1, where one day He's healing all kinds of people." With a twinkle in his eye, Vince said, "I got the feeling the disciples thought this could be a good business. The next day a big crowd was going to gather to get more of the same, but then something happened. Can you quote that passage?"

"Not quite," said Mike. "But I've got my Bible right here." He pulled it from his briefcase and opened to Mark 1:35–38: "Very early in the morning, while it was still dark, Jesus got up, left the house and went off to a solitary place, where he prayed. Simon and his companions went to look for him, and when they found him, they exclaimed: 'Everyone is looking for you!' Jesus replied, 'Let us go somewhere else—to the nearby villages—so I can preach there also. That is why I have come.'"

"What does that say to you about the habits of Jesus?" Vince asked.

"His habit of solitude empowered Him to stay on purpose and follow God's will rather than do the popular thing," replied Mike. "This passage shows that Jesus had the same temptations we all have—being busy, getting caught up in events, and losing sight of the big picture."

Vince nodded. "Yes, and it shows why it's important to have habits that keep us focused and moving ahead on God's plan rather than our own."

The captain broke into their conversation, announcing that the plane was approaching their destination and asking everyone to return the tray tables to their full and upright position.

"Thanks, Vince," said Mike. "I really appreciate all the insights you've given me to think about."

"I sure hope your *friend* finds them helpful," Vince said. "This world—and especially your friend's line of business—needs more leaders who are leading like Jesus." Vince pulled out his wallet and extracted a business card, which he handed to Mike. "If your friend ever needs any further advice, just have him give me a call," he said with a smile.

"Both my friend and I appreciate your kindness," said Mike, laughing.

Before the plane landed, Mike summarized what he had learned from Vince:

❤ Jesus is the greatest leadership role model of all time.

❤ Leadership is an influence process. Anytime you're engaged in influencing the thinking, behavior, or development of others, you're engaged in leadership.

♥ Leadership is not just about positions. There are organizational leadership roles and life leadership roles.

♥ Effective servant leadership is first a matter of character and intention. Are you leading to serve or to be served?

♥ Daily habits of solitude, prayer, and application of Scripture help you to stay focused on being a true servant leader.

Chapter 13

THE LEADER JESUS
HAD IN MIND

Mike and Jane stood in the baggage claim area, watching for their bags to appear on the conveyer belt.

"Sounds like you were having quite a lively conversation with your seatmate on the plane," she said. "I didn't want to disturb you, but I sure enjoyed eavesdropping."

"Wasn't he something?" commented Mike. "I really appreciated Vince's input. And it's amazing because it gave me the other piece I was missing. I spent my sabbatical getting clear on the church Jesus had in mind. But getting clear on His vision left me in a quandary about how to make that happen at Beacon Hill. The thing I needed was guidance on the kind of leadership that Jesus had in mind. Enter Vince, thank God. As always, God's never late but always on time!"

Later that night, after they had unpacked their luggage and settled back into their routine, Mike spent some time in his study looking into the leadership that Jesus envisioned for His church. The first thing he confirmed from his conversation with Vince was that Jesus did indeed want His church to be led by servant leaders.

But whenever Mike mentioned servant leadership to lay-people, they thought the term meant *the inmates are running the prison* or *the leader is trying to please everyone.* He knew that was not what Jesus had in mind.

As he dove into the Gospels, he realized that when Jesus talked about servant leadership, there were two parts: vision and implementation.

Mike had learned that a compelling vision told people who they were, where they were going, and what would guide their journey. In Matthew 4:19, when He called His first disciples, Jesus said, "Come, follow me, and I will make you fishers of men." That was clearly *who* Jesus wanted His disciples to be. In Matthew 28:19, Jesus signaled *where* He wanted His disciples to go. He charged them to "go and make disciples of all nations, baptizing them in the name of the Father and of the Son and of the Holy Spirit." When it came to *what* would guide their journey, Jesus made that clear as well:

"'Love the Lord your God with all your heart and with all your soul and with all your mind.' This is the first and greatest commandment. And the second is like it: 'Love your neighbor as yourself.' All the Law and the Prophets hang on these two commandments."

—Matthew 22: 37–40

It became clear to Mike that vision was the *leadership* part of servant leadership and implementation was the *servant* aspect. In John 13:12–15, Jesus modeled being a servant when He washed the feet of the disciples:

When he had finished washing their feet, he put on his clothes and returned to his place. "Do you understand what I have done for you?" he asked them. "You call me 'Teacher' and 'Lord,' and rightly so, for that is what I am. Now that I, your Lord and Teacher, have washed your feet, you also should wash one another's feet. I have set you an example that you should do as I have done for you."

It seemed obvious to Mike that when it came to the implementation of His vision, Jesus wanted His disciples to focus on the servant part of servant leadership.

Mike realized that the traditional hierarchy is good for the visionary aspect of leadership. After all, Jesus got His vision from the top of the hierarchy—His Father. However, effective implementation required turning the hierarchy upside down and putting the leader at the bottom, serving those with the responsibility to manifest the vision. That's what Jesus was doing when He washed the feet of His disciples.

Mike knew what this meant for his future leadership of Beacon Hill. It would be his responsibility, along with the elders, to set the vision for any necessary change. Once that was done, he and the elders would need to become cheerleaders and supporters of all those who were to make the vision a reality.

Mike looked up from his desk and rubbed his eyes. This was enough thinking for one day. He shook his head as he realized that for him to be the servant leader Jesus wanted him to be, he was going to have to get out of his own way. He said a silent prayer as he got up from the desk:

Lord, clean me out of me, fill me up with You, and then clothe me with humility.

Chapter 14

A MEETING OF HEARTS
AND MINDS

Tim Manning was seated on a bench outside the church administration office when Pastor Mike arrived for their meeting the next morning. When Mike called to set up this meeting, Tim felt relieved. Now he had the perfect opening to talk with Mike about the loss of love in the church.

"Welcome back, my friend," said Tim as he rose to greet Mike. "How was the sabbatical?" Tim's smile hid the concern he felt inside about how Mike might react to the criticism contained in the letter he had folded in his pocket. He anticipated that Mike might take on too much of the responsibility for what had happened. Having taken his ego issues before the

Lord and forgiving himself, Tim hoped he could help Mike develop perspective about the unhappy news he was about to deliver.

"You look rested," Tim observed.

"I am," replied Mike. "Not only am I rested; I'm inspired. I had a real breakthrough about the church while I was away."

"So did I," said Tim.

"Before we go inside, let's pray," Mike suggested.

Pastor Mike prayed, "Heavenly Father, thank You for bringing us together this morning to open up a new chapter in the life of Beacon Hill Community Church. Thank You for the opportunity You have provided us to care for Your people. Bless my friend Tim and our time together, that we might glorify You by being about Your business. In Jesus' name, amen."

As he listened to Pastor Mike's prayer, Tim was stunned by the words *open up a new chapter in the life of Beacon Hill Community Church.* He, too, envisioned a new chapter in the life of the church. But what it would look like and how it would be made into a positive reality were questions Tim had only begun to contemplate. He did know that this new chapter would require a lot of soul-searching, humility, and courage on the part of the Beacon Hill leadership team, beginning with himself and Pastor Mike.

"So besides that great tan, what are you bringing back from your sabbatical?" Tim asked.

Mike said, "I spent two months exploring the question:

What was the church that Jesus had in mind as opposed to what we have today?"

"What was the big *aha*?" asked Tim.

"That by focusing on the love of God and one another, we can become the church that Jesus had in mind for us. That church is first and foremost a loving community. That's an exciting vision, but I had no idea how to make it happen. Then yesterday I had the most amazing encounter on the plane, and through that, God helped me fill in the blanks," replied Mike.

"What happened?" asked Tim.

As he led Tim into his office, Mike said, "A man on the plane—a business writer of all things—and I got into a conversation about the leadership of Jesus." Mike slipped behind his desk and sat down. "It's my hope, Tim, that before you leave the council, we can help the church become that loving community by leading like Jesus."

Tim lowered himself into the guest chair and gradually began to comprehend the miracle that was unfolding. With all of his concerns leading up to this meeting, he never anticipated that the Holy Spirit would have been preparing Pastor Mike's heart and mind to lead the church on the journey to recovery that was so vital to its future. As Tim's fears turned to joy, he smiled and shook his head in awe.

"Gee, Tim," said Pastor Mike, "I don't know what I said that is causing you to smile, but I hope it isn't because you think I've lost my marbles!"

"Not at all," replied Tim. "In fact, I'm stunned by how God has been preparing and equipping us for this moment. I'm blown away by how much He loves His church. You see, He's been leading me on a quest that's ultimately all about creating the loving community you've been thinking about." The smile disappeared from Tim's face. "Sometimes it's been tough."

"What's been going on?"

"It all started when I received a letter three weeks ago. That began the learning journey."

"What did it say?" asked Mike.

Tim pulled the letter from his pocket and read it aloud, emphasizing key passages: "You and Beacon Hill Community Church have drifted away from the love of God and one another as your first priority."

When he was finished, Tim handed the letter across the desk to Pastor Mike.

Mike stared down at the letter in his hands. "It's amazing how much this letter has in common with Jesus' letter in the book of Revelation to the church at Ephesus. This one is signed 'Your Truest Friend.' Any idea who really sent it?"

Tim smiled and shook his head. "At first I thought it was from one of the chronic critics at the church. I was going to blow it off, but then I got a phone call from a young woman named Dani, who told me she was leaving the church. Her reasons tracked precisely with the charges laid out in the letter," Tim said. "Something she said really summed it up. She said that Beacon Hill wasn't exactly the most loving place in town."

"Ouch," said Pastor Mike.

"Ouch is right," echoed Tim. "At that point I knew I needed help. I went to my mentor and friend, Hank Dalton, who sent me to a number of people for counsel. God also sent a variety of teachers to me, from a baby to an old nemesis. Every encounter was a lesson in love, faith, and forgiveness," he concluded.

"I guess I shouldn't be amazed by these miracles," said Pastor Mike. "After all, when He first laid claim to His church, Jesus said, 'On this rock I will build my church, and the gates of Hades will not overcome it' [Matt. 16:18].

"I don't know about you, Tim," said Mike, "but it seems to me we are onto something pretty important on God's agenda for Beacon Hill."

"It sure feels that way to me," replied Tim. "And it seems to be God's plan for us to walk through this testing time together."

"I'm glad Jesus promises in Matthew 18:20 that when two or three come together in His name, He will be there with them," Mike said. "If we're going to lead the church back to what He had in mind, we're going to have to stay closely attached to Him and to one another. And, Tim, I'm not sure how to proceed. What we are facing is way beyond anything I have ever experienced, and I'm uncertain about where to begin."

"From what I've been learning over the past several weeks," answered Tim, "I think the way to start is by keeping prayer as our first response rather than our last resort."

"Great idea," replied Pastor Mike. "Why don't you begin?"

After a moment of quiet reflection, Tim began to pray: "Father God, I am in awe and humbled by how You have been preparing Pastor Mike and me to be part of restoring the love priority You have set in place for Your church. Father, this task is beyond anything we can imagine accomplishing outside of Your help. Bind us together in mind and spirit. Help us to trust each other as we put our trust in You. In Jesus' name, amen."

Pastor Mike then prayed, "Heavenly Father, thank You for Your mercy and forgiveness. Thank You for waking us from our complacency and blindness so we can renew a loving relationship with You and restore love to the church. I pray that Your forgiving and active love will be our model. Guide us each step of the way back to You. In Jesus' name we pray, amen."

As Mike finished his prayer, the word *love* and all its promise filled Tim's mind. "I think I know where God wants us to begin," he said. "To put it into the words that Dani used, I think we are being called to make Beacon Hill the most loving place in town."

Chapter 15

LOVE-BASED LEADERSHIP

"It's all there in 1 Corinthians 13," said Tim. "Without love, nothing's going to work, no matter how brilliant we think our ideas might be. Love is the common denominator in both what Jesus had in mind for His church and how it's to be accomplished."

Pastor Mike agreed: "What the Holy Spirit seems to be calling us to do is to lead a love revival at Beacon Hill Community Church! The biggest question I have is *how*. I know my preaching and teaching from the pulpit will play a part in communicating the vision and values of the church that Jesus had in mind, but it won't be enough. Lasting change is going to require a lot more than proclamation. It's going to require demonstration over the long haul."

"That's where we're really going to have to be servant leaders," replied Tim. "This task is way beyond anything that can be accomplished by one person alone. Our next step will have to be getting the entire Elder Council on board with the vision of Beacon Hill as the most loving place in town. That's going to take a multitude of people supporting one another with love-based motivation, thinking, behavior, and habits."

"Vince Blakely opened my eyes to the fact that Jesus was the greatest leadership role model of all time," noted Pastor Mike. "He explained to me that Jesus modeled servant leadership in four dimensions—the heart, the head, the hands, and the habits. And one thing he made crystal clear is that if the heart doesn't stay right, the rest falls apart."

Tim said, "Boy, I can relate to that. Since I got that letter, I've been battling three things—pride, fear, and denial. I think we'll have to continually battle them as we try to make this happen. When we go public with this letter—and I think we should—false pride and fear are going to rear their ugly heads. We need to plan how to stay on track."

"I'm not entirely certain what God has in mind to revive the church," said Pastor Mike. "But whatever we do going forward, we need to keep Jesus in the middle of it. Jesus left no doubt about what would happen to the efforts of even His most ardent admirers and enthusiastic workers when they went about doing things on their own." He reached for the Bible in Tim's hands and opened it to John 15:5: "Apart from me you can do *nothing*."

"*Nothing* is a very intense word," said Tim. "It sure doesn't leave any room for argument or wiggle room to justify going it alone."

"The problems we're having at Beacon Hill were anticipated by Jesus," Pastor Mike pointed out. "When Jesus first issued the command to serve rather than be served, even His divine influence didn't restrain His disciples' ambitions. Remember how they argued about who would get the seat of honor in His kingdom?"

Mike turned to Luke 22:24–26 and read about the dispute that arose among the disciples as to which one of them would be regarded as the greatest. "Here's that servant leadership directive again," said Mike, reading the words of Jesus: "The greatest among you should be like the youngest, and the one who rules like the one who serves."

"It's kind of comforting to see that there's nothing new under the sun in the challenges of the human heart," said Tim. "All this pride and fear—all this bitterness and division—is really nothing new."

"And all the old remedies of prayer, repentance, apology, compassion, kindness, patience, truthfulness, and love still retain their potency," said Pastor Mike.

"I just thought of another passage about leadership and

love," said Tim. "May I?" he asked, holding his hands out for the Bible. When Mike handed it over, Tim turned to John 21:15–17 and read:

Jesus said to Simon Peter, "Simon son of John, do you truly love me more than these?"

"Yes, Lord," he said, "you know that I love you."

Jesus said, "Feed my lambs."

Again Jesus said, "Simon son of John, do you truly love me?"

He answered, "Yes, Lord, you know that I love you."

Jesus said, "Take care of my sheep."

The third time he said to him, "Simon son of John, do you love me?"

Peter was hurt because Jesus asked him the third time, "Do you love me?" He said, "Lord, you know all things; you know that I love you."

Jesus said, "Feed my sheep."

"So unless we're loving others—feeding His sheep—we're not showing our love for Jesus," noted Pastor Mike.

"That's right," said Tim. "Which reminds me. There's one thing I can do right now on a personal level to feed one of His sheep."

"What's that?" Pastor Mike asked.

"I'm going to call Dani Wilson, the lamb our church seems to have left behind," said Tim. "I want to reassure her that despite the behavior of some members, she really is welcome at Beacon Hill. I also want to tell her about our goal to make Beacon Hill the most loving place in town. Even if she doesn't want to return, at least I can let her know we care."

Chapter 16

THE CHALLENGE OF CHANGE

Pastor Mike was back in his study, alternately praying about the new vision for the church and grappling with how to make it happen. The magnitude of change was beyond anything he had ever attempted before. He could feel one of his old enemies—fear of failure—breathing down his neck.

Who do you think you are that you're going to be able to pull this off? The reality is, you're going to crash and burn, and take a lot of people with you.

There they were again, his old enemies of pride and fear. He was coming down with his Superman syndrome again. Right away, the antidote came to mind. He turned to Philippians 4:6–8:

Do not be anxious about anything, but in everything,

by prayer and petition, with thanksgiving, present your requests to God. And the peace of God, which transcends all understanding, will guard your hearts and your minds in Christ Jesus. Finally, brothers, whatever is true, whatever is noble, whatever is right, whatever is pure, whatever is lovely, whatever is admirable—if anything is excellent or praiseworthy—think about such things.

Mike bowed his head and prayed for help.

The help came in the form of a thought. No sooner had he said "amen" than Vince Blakely's friendly face came to mind. Mike smiled and decided to take Vince up on his offer to help a friend in need.

He went to his desk, fumbled through his papers, and found Vince's card. He dialed the number, and to his surprise, Vince's booming voice answered the phone.

"This is Pastor Mike from the airplane," he said. "I bet you didn't expect to get a call from me this quickly. But my friend is in trouble and could really use your guidance."

"Fire away. A friend of yours is a friend of mine," Vince said warmly.

"Okay, on a serious note, let me share my situation," said Mike. He went on to tell Vince about the letter that his head elder had received and the new vision that he had developed during his sabbatical. "Bottom line, Vince, is that a huge change is necessary at our church, and it's bigger than we know how to handle. We need help."

"What I've found out over the years, Mike, is that a need for change occurs when there's a difference between what's actually happening and what you want to have happen. It seems to me you're getting all the signals that you've been a very busy, activity-oriented church, and what God and your members are looking for is a more loving church."

"Exactly," agreed Mike. "But how do we get there from here?"

"Start slowly," said Vince. "The biggest problem I've found with change agents is that when they first present their vision for change, they immediately want to talk about benefits and why it's going to be so much better for everyone. Research has shown that that's about the fourth or fifth concern of people. The first thing they want is information. So I think you and Tim need to lay out the facts—owning your part of the problem as well as your anxieties about fixing it."

"As the head pastor, I feel completely responsible," Mike said. "Is that what I should share?"

"Probably, but one caution: if you set it up as all your fault, it's all yours to fix. The truth is, everyone has a role in this, and everyone will have a role in making it better.

"Second, I think you're on the right track because it sounds like you have a clear vision of where you want to go. All lasting change starts with clear vision and direction."

"I think we're on the right track too," said Mike. "Jesus was certainly clear about His vision of being a loving community when He said in John's gospel, 'A new command I give you: Love one another. As I have loved you, so you must love one another. By this all men will know that you are my disciples' [13:34–35]."

"Okay, love-based leadership is your vision," said Vince. "Once people understand what you have in mind, you have to give them a chance to deal with their personal concerns about the change. How will they fit in? How can they contribute? I recommend you set up mourning sessions where people can mourn the old ways because I guarantee some of your congregation are benefiting from the busyness and have wrapped their egos around the performance of 'good works.'"

"Why is this a necessary step?" asked Mike.

"Because in life, what you resist, persists. If you don't give people an avenue to express their concerns, they'll gunnysack them and unload them later."

"We certainly don't want that," said Mike.

"No, you don't," said Vince. "If people get a chance to deal with what's bothering them, in the process their concerns often go away. Have you ever said to yourself, 'I'm glad I got that off my chest'?"

"I sure have," said Mike. "And getting things off my chest does help put my concerns behind me."

"During this process, sharing your own vulnerability and

past regrets is absolutely essential," Vince stated. "For people to buy into a change, they have to know that you're committed to the change and are making sacrifices too."

"You mean I have to be vulnerable?"

"You betcha," said Vince. "What's your biggest concern?"

"My biggest concern at this point is that I'm not sure I can see my way through turning this from vision to reality. I don't know if I have the skills to create the implementation plan that will work."

"It's interesting you mention that," said Vince. "Because the next concern people have is implementation. They want to know what's going to happen first, second, and third. The more detail you give them, the better."

"You're making me even more nervous about my lack of skills in this area," said Mike.

"You don't have to do it all on your own. In fact, if your ego keeps you from bringing others into the process, you will remain isolated from resources available to you. This is the point where you raise your hand and ask for help," Vince explained.

"Maybe at this point I can bring in the church elders," suggested Mike, "so that they can help me come up with the implementation plan for making Beacon Hill the most loving place in town."

"You're going to have to reinforce the vision and values over and over again. The big picture, Mike, is that effective change is more about managing the journey than announcing the destination."

"I think I've got it," said Mike. "Thanks for your help."

"Hold on. One last suggestion," added Vince. "I heard you on the plane and again just now talk about fear and pride. Those are ego problems. I recommend that at some point you hold an Egos Anonymous meeting with your top leaders."

"Egos Anonymous! That's a good one," said Mike.

"I think it's more than appropriate," said Vince, "because fear- and pride-based ego is behind all addictions. Fear comes from thinking less of yourself than you should. Fear can lead people into abuse of drugs, alcohol, overeating, and other negative addictions they think can make them feel good about themselves in the short run. With false pride, people think more of themselves than they should, which can lead them to focus too much on accumulation of wealth, recognition, power, and status. Both fear and false pride cause people to focus on themselves. They think, *It's all about me.* They Edge God Out and forget that they are unconditionally loved. Admitting this is the first step to recovery. Without recovery from an out-of-control ego, you can never lead like Jesus."

With that, Vince told Mike exactly how to run an Egos Anonymous meeting.

After he hung up the phone, a profound peace came over Pastor Mike. He smiled as he realized that even when his self-esteem was at its lowest and he was cowering in the brutal light of honesty about his failings, he should know that he was always loved and important to his heavenly Father. He laughed as he thought, *If I could develop the habit of accepting the unconditional love of our Father, I wouldn't have much to confess at an Egos Anonymous meeting!*

The more Pastor Mike thought about it, the more he realized that ego issues of pride and fear were going to be the biggest barriers to restoring love of God and one another to the church. If love was to be the antidote for what was missing at Beacon Hill, both he and Tim would need to lead the way in combating the ego issues that were bound to emerge.

Inspired by his vision of returning Beacon Hill to the kind of church that Jesus had in mind, Pastor Mike telephoned Tim, and they agreed to call a special meeting of the elders for the following Monday night.

That done, he summarized his new learnings from his conversation with Vince:

- ♥ All lasting change starts with clear vision and direction.

- ♥ The first thing people want to know when faced with change is information.

- ♥ The next thing they have are personal concerns—they want to know how the change will affect them.

♥ Once people's personal concerns are dealt with, they want to know what the implementation plans are—what will happen first, second, third, and so on.

♥ After these concerns have been dealt with, people are more open to hear about the benefits of the change.

♥ When implementing change, you don't have to do it all on your own.

♥ Developing a strategy to deal with fear and pride issues is important in any change effort.

Chapter 17

LOVE REVEALED

Tim Manning wanted to be prepared for the Monday night Elder Council meeting. He was eager to assist Pastor Mike in leading others to restore love to the church. One thing that still puzzled him, though, was how to describe in practical terms the love of God and one another that the church so desperately needed. *Love* was such a broad concept, a word that had been sadly misused and trivialized. Unless they were clear about what they were asking for, it would be hard for them to guide others toward that goal.

It was Saturday afternoon when Tim got some unexpected help in answering his question. Looking through the afternoon mail, he found a slim book-sized package from

Clair Bowen among the bills and junk mail. Inside was a brief note that read:

Dear Tim,

Thank you again for your encouraging visit. I have been praying for you ever since. I also prayed for God to reveal to me any way I could be of help to you. He answered my prayer by reminding me of a book I had read a long time ago. It speaks to the heart of the issue of Christian love in a way I had never seen before or since. I hope it blesses your journey, as it has mine.

Resting in His holy arms, your sister in Christ,

Clair

The book from Clair was *The Greatest Thing in the World,* written by the nineteenth-century Scottish evangelist Henry Drummond, with an introduction by Dwight L. Moody. Moody was so impressed with its message that he'd requested the principals of the schools he had founded to read it to the student body once a year.

The book was a powerful analysis of love as the greatest thing in the world—and it was based on 1 Corinthians 13. It described nine components of love:

1. Patience
2. Kindness

3. Generosity

4. Courtesy

5. Humility

6. Unselfishness

7. Good temper

8. Guilelessness

9. Sincerity

If Beacon Hill Community Church was to be, as Pastor Mike and he had envisioned, the most loving place in town, these elements of love should permeate the relationships of its people. It occurred to Tim that these attributes would be a perfect way for the church leaders to assess their hearts.

In preparation for the council meeting, Tim developed a brief questionnaire to present to the elders that would measure the current status of love in their relationships. He hoped his questionnaire—based on the thoughts expressed by Henry Drummond—would help others gain a deeper understanding as well.

NINE COMPONENTS OF LOVE QUESTIONNAIRE

1. *Patience:* Love as patience endures evil, injury, and provocation without being filled with resentment, indignation, or

revenge. It will put up with many slights and neglects from the person it loves and wait long to see the kindly effects of such patience on him.

When do I demonstrate love as patience?
When do I struggle to demonstrate love as patience?

2. *Kindness*: Love as kindness is active. Kindness seeks to be useful. It not only seizes on opportunities for doing good but also searches for them.

When do I express love as kindness?
When do I struggle with expressing love as kindness?

3. *Generosity*: Love as generosity does not envy the good fortune or accomplishments of others. If we love our neighbor, we will be so far from envying her and what she possesses or accomplishes that we will share in it and rejoice at it. The prosperity of those to whom we wish well can never grieve us.

When do I express love as generosity?
When do I struggle with expressing love as generosity?

4. *Courtesy*: Love as courtesy is love in the little things. It behaves toward all people with goodwill. It seeks to promote

the *happiness* of all. It avoids profane and indecent language and coarse and vulgar expressions that pain the ear and offend the hearts of others.

When do I exhibit love as courtesy?
When do I struggle to exhibit love as courtesy?

5. *Humility*: Love as humility does not promote or call attention to itself, is not puffed up, is not bloated with self-conceit, and does not dwell upon its accomplishments. When true brotherly love is exhibited, we will find things to praise in others and will esteem others.

When do I express love as humility?
When do I struggle with expressing love as humility?

6. *Unselfishness*: Love as unselfishness never seeks its own to the harm or disadvantage of others, or with the neglect of others. It often neglects its own for the sake of others; it prefers their welfare, satisfaction, and advantage to its own; and it ever prefers the good of the community to its private advantage. It would not advance, aggrandize, enrich, or gratify itself at the cost and damage of the public.

When do I express love as unselfishness?
When do I struggle to express love as unselfishness?

7. *Good temper:* Love as good temper restrains the passions and is not exasperated. It corrects a sharpness of temper and sweetens and softens attitudes. Love as good temper is never angry without a cause and endeavors to confine the passions within proper limits. Anger cannot rest in the heart where love reigns. It is hard to be angry with loved ones in good temper but very easy to drop resentments and be reconciled.

   When do I exhibit love as good temper?
   When do I struggle to exhibit love as good temper?

8. *Guilelessness:* Love as guilelessness thinks no evil, suspects no ill motive, sees the bright side, and puts the best construction on every action. It is grace for suspicious people. It cherishes no malice; it does not give way to revenge. It is not apt to be jealous and suspicious.

   When do I model love as guilelessness?
   When do I struggle to model love as guilelessness?

9. *Sincerity:* Love as sincerity takes no pleasure in doing injury or hurt to others or broadcasting their seeming miscues. It speaks only what is known to be true, necessary, and edifying. It bears no false witness and does not gossip. It rejoices in the truth.

When do I demonstrate love as sincerity?

When do I struggle to demonstrate love as sincerity?

As Tim reviewed the questionnaire, he was again struck with a sense of amazement at how he was personally being guided into a deeper understanding of what it meant to abide in the love of God and His people. He also realized that love is lived out in the day-to-day choices people make in their relationships with each other.

He reflected on the upcoming meeting. *The days ahead should be interesting,* he thought.

Chapter 18

CALLING IN THE ELDERS

A subtle tension filled the air as the members of the Beacon Hill Elder Council gathered in the church conference room. Ever since attendance and the church financial picture had improved, Tim Manning rarely called special meetings of the council. When he did, the news was rarely positive. That was probably why the elders were unusually quiet as Tim called the meeting to order.

"Thank you for rearranging your schedules to be here this evening," said Tim after the opening prayer. "As you know, I have avoided calling special meetings unless there was something of vital importance that we, as a leadership team, needed to address. This is one of those times. What I have to say will in the beginning seem extremely discouraging to you, as it did to me. But I encourage you to withhold judgment until both Pastor Mike and I have finished telling you what has become clear to us about a vision for the future at Beacon Hill Community Church."

Tim then read to the elders the letter he had received. He described his initial stunned reaction and feelings of disbelief about the claim that their church had abandoned love of God and love of one another as their first priority.

"Then I got a disturbing phone call," said Tim. He went on to describe his call from Dani and how her comments tracked with the shortcomings the letter had described. He talked about his journey in coming to grips with these events and starting on the road back to making love a top priority at Beacon Hill.

The conference room had gotten quiet. Sensing the elders' somber mood, Tim ended his remarks with a ray of encouragement.

"The author of this letter told me the plain truth in a way that was more redirecting and hope filled than condemning and despairing," Tim said. "Although the letter gave me a bleak picture of my leadership, I found comfort in the phrase 'all is not lost.' It gave me hope that through the grace of God, what had been lost could be restored. It reaffirmed to me that even when my attention and passion had drifted into the things that pride and fear made important, God's love for me and for His church never wavered or lost its intensity. I became convinced again that if, as my brother Charlie Duck had suggested, I admitted I was broken and let God do the fixing, I could finish the work He had given me to do.

"It was with this thought in mind," Tim continued, "that I went to meet with Pastor Mike on the day he returned from his sabbatical. I must admit that I wasn't looking forward to laying on Mike such a serious, negative assessment of the current state of the church—especially on his first day back on the job. But as it turned out, my fears turned into great joy when Mike told me what God had been doing in his life at the same time. Here is where things get really exciting. I'm now going to turn the floor over to Pastor Mike and have him tell you his part of this pretty amazing story of God at work."

Pastor Mike then told the elders about his journey, including his "chance" encounter on the airplane with Vince Blakely, the business author who'd affirmed that Jesus was the greatest leadership role model of all time. The mood in the room lightened considerably as Pastor Mike outlined the kind of leaders Jesus had called all of them to be and read his loving vision for the church.

Now the room hummed with excitement as the elders began talking among themselves. Rick Reardon, one of the newest elders, raised his hand.

"Yes, Rick," said Pastor Mike. "Please share your thoughts."

"I just want to thank you for wanting to get this place back on track. I joined the church to love God and His family, not to argue with other church members about what kind of audiovisual equipment to install in the main chapel."

The room filled with laughter.

"Seriously," Rick continued, "sometimes it's felt like the audiovisual equipment was more important than the people. I'm excited about our new focus."

"Thanks for your enthusiasm, Rick," said Mike.

Steve Alvarez, one of the longtime members of the church, spoke up: "I agree that a change in direction might be needed, but it is not going to be easy. We have a rich history at Beacon Hill of providing excellent programs and services to our congregation and the community. Our people take pride in these things. Some folks who've invested a lot of years into making our church the very best it can be may resent being told that they have been led down the wrong path."

"Thanks, Steve. I appreciate the reality check," responded Pastor Mike. "We need to be clear among ourselves as a leadership team what we want to continue to celebrate about Beacon Hill as it is today and what we want to leave behind. Before we jump into what's ahead, let's take stock of what we're seeking to leave behind. By moving to a more loving church, is there anything we are going to mourn having to give up? For example, I'm not going to be able to hold grudges anymore, and the two-year-old brat in me kind of resents that."

The elders laughed.

With Pastor Mike's example leading the way, Tim asked the elders to break into pairs and talk about anything they might be concerned about giving up as they moved the church toward being the most loving place in town. The room initially was filled with laughter, but the atmosphere became more subdued as everyone got down to the brutal honesty of mourning the loss of the status quo.

Tim wandered around the room to get a sense of how everyone was doing. When he realized that the conversations were winding down, he again focused everyone's energy toward the front of the room.

"Why don't we share the concerns you came up with. Just call them out," Tim said. "What are you going to mourn or miss?"

"I'm going to miss the freedom to be self-centered and decide whether I'm going to be pleasant or not," one elder volunteered.

"I'm going to mourn giving up busyness as a badge of honor because I've become a real pro at it!" said another.

"I'm going to miss using church attendance just for getting a quick spiritual fix on the weekends and as part of my 'good person' to-do list," said another.

"I'm going to miss looking down on people who don't know the Bible as well as I do or put in as much time as I do in active church work," said another.

"That's good," Tim said. "These are great. Anyone else?"

"I guess I'm going to miss hiding behind telling people, 'I'll pray for you,' as my response to their problems because I don't want to spend the time to really give them the ongoing help they need," stated another.

"With all due respect to Pastor Mike," said an older member of the council, "I'm going to miss critiquing the quality of his sermons and worship services based on how well my preferences are being met rather than on what they reveal about my walk with the Lord."

Tim listened until all of the elders had shared. There were some good laughs throughout. "It sounds from your laughter that you're beginning to recognize that the familiarity of the past—even if it's undesirable—is a lot less scary than the unknown future."

Around the room, heads nodded.

"Before we try to identify the benefits of becoming the most loving place in town, I have some homework for you."

A few groans were heard around the room.

"This won't be too painful," Tim promised, "because it's about love. I'm going to ask each of you to read 1 Corinthians 13 over the next twenty-four hours. Then I want you to spend some time in prayer and reflection, contemplating which aspect of love described in that chapter you've fallen short of when interacting with your brothers and sisters at Beacon Hill Community Church."

"Will there be a quiz?" Rick asked jokingly.

"In a way, yes," replied Tim. He handed a stack of questionnaires to Rick and motioned for him to distribute them to the other elders. "After you read 1 Corinthians 13, fill out this questionnaire. I also want you to search for these specific components of love in the various aspects of your ministries. For example, if you work in the parking ministry, how is love showing up there? If you have a Bible study, how are you doing at expressing love there? Write down your answers and be prepared to report them at the annual elders' retreat that's scheduled for next weekend."

Grousing good-naturedly about their homework assignment, the elders rose from their seats and began filing from the room.

Chapter 19

TAKING INVENTORY

The annual elders' retreat was held at the YMCA retreat center outside of town. It wasn't fancy, but it was perfect for the soul-searching work that lay ahead.

Pastor Mike and the elders gathered in the main conference room. After they settled into their seats, Tim said, "Okay, it's confession time. Let's hear how love did on your questionnaires. Who wants to start?"

"I found love as *patience* among the volunteer nursery workers in my group," said one elder.

Another elder laughed and said, "I didn't find patience in my work with our business office. Sometimes we act like we're working for General Motors rather than Beacon Hill Community Church!"

"I found love as *generosity* in the missions ministry," said another elder. "There are a lot of servant hearts over there. That's why I love that ministry."

"I wish I found more generosity in my weekly Bible study," stated one elder. "When I took a hard look, I found jealousy toward the folks who really knew the Bible."

"How about humility?" Tim asked.

"I looked for it in hospitality services," offered one elder. "But what I found instead was boastfulness when things went well and defensiveness when suggestions for improvement came our way."

Tim went one by one through each of the characteristics, hearing some positive stories as well as negative ones. "I'm really inspired by your examples of where love reigns," said Tim. "But I'm disheartened by where we fall short."

One elder who was typically quiet rose to his feet and said, "What I got out of this discussion is that we need to be leaders, not just snoopy reporters. If we want to restore the love that has been lost in this church, we have to search our hearts and find ways to make the 'loving thing' our single leadership priority."

"What I hear you saying," said Tim, "is the old Pogo quote, 'We have met the enemy, and he is us.'"

With a grin on his face, Pastor Mike stood up and said,

"Tim, I can't think of a better time than now to hold the first Beacon Hill Egos Anonymous meeting." A few bursts of laughter were heard throughout the conference room.

Continuing on, Pastor Mike said, "As in all twelve-step programs, the first step is owning up to the problem. This may be awkward at first and a little scary, but if we can take this first step together, we can start to break down some barriers to healing our hearts and spirits.

"The second step to recovery is acknowledging that only through the work of a higher power, which we rightly name as God, can true recovery be attained. To this end," continued Mike, "I'd like to open this next portion of our time together with a prayer of invitation for the Holy Spirit to guide us in a time of trust and transparency."

Mike offered a brief prayer, which he concluded by quoting King David's plea in Psalm 51:10 (ESV): "Create in me a clean heart, O God, and renew a right spirit within me."

With that, Mike asked the elders to stand up behind their chairs. "As many of you know from AA and other twelve-step programs, the meetings are voluntary. If you've never been bitten by false pride or fear, feel free to leave and come back in a half hour. But remember, that means you've never whined when you weren't given the recognition you thought you deserved, and you've never been shut down by your fear of inadequacy. Any takers?"

No one moved a muscle.

"All right, let's sit down and begin our meeting. For any of you who are familiar with twelve-step programs, our format will be similar," said Mike. "What you'll do is stand up and introduce yourself by saying, 'Hi, my name is (blank).' Everyone will greet you. Then you'll say, 'I'm an egomaniac. The last time my ego got in the way was . . .' Here you'll give an example of a bout with false pride or fear. After people have shared, let's all give them a hand."

There was an awkward pause as all the elders waited for someone else to go first.

"Since I brought it up, let me go first," said Pastor Mike as he stood up. "Hi, my name is Mike."

"Hi, Mike," everyone chimed in.

"I'm an egomaniac. The last time my ego got in the way was before my wife, Jane, and I returned from my sabbatical. I was carrying the weight of the entire church family on my shoulders until Jane told me to leave my Superman complex behind and admit that my skills were in preaching and sharing the gospel, and not necessarily in leading the whole church all by myself." As Mike sat down, everyone applauded.

The next person to stand up was Tim Manning. "Hi, my name is Tim."

"Hi, Tim," the group responded.

"I'm an egomaniac, and my biggest ego challenge comes in the form of fear. I feared rejection and failure when I was confronted with the fact that my leadership had contributed to the church's drifting off course. My first reaction was to deny the truth and keep the letter I'd received a secret. But I did get my ego out of the way long enough to pray and to ask for help."

As Tim Manning sat down to the affirming applause of the group, Steve Alvarez stood and said, "Hi, my name is Steve."

"Hi, Steve," the group said in a chorus.

"I'm an egomaniac because I constantly struggle with my ego in meetings when I think I'm the only one in the room who knows the right answer to a problem."

After Steve spoke, another elder raised his hand, followed by another. The confessions poured out until nearly every elder had spoken. The room grew silent.

Sensing that everyone who wanted to speak had done so, Tim addressed the group: "Thank you for joining in on this exercise. Its purpose was to let each of us know that we won't be alone in experiencing challenges of the heart as we seek to lead the church to a higher level. Someone once said that when you name your demons, they start to lose their power. I think it's true. When we recognize and name those aspects of our individual and collective character that keep us from being instruments of God's love, they start to dry up and blow away. By telling the truth and yielding our hearts and wills to God, we receive the power and grace to love one another the way Jesus had in mind.

"For the rest of the morning I'd like us to find quiet spots for individual prayer and reflection. Let's scatter throughout the property. Before you go, let me leave you with some thoughts from 1 John 4:7–12 and 1 John 4:19–21."

He opened his Bible and read:

Dear friends, let us love one another, for love comes from God. Everyone who loves has been born of God and knows God. Whoever does not love does not know God, because God is love. This is how God showed his love among us: He sent his one and only Son into the world that we might live through him. This is love: not that we loved God, but that he loved us and sent his Son as an atoning sacrifice for our sins. Dear friends, since God so loved us, we also ought to love one another. No one has ever seen God; but if we love one another, God lives in us and his love is made complete in us.

Turning to the next verses, he read:

We love because he first loved us. If anyone says, "I love God," yet hates his brother, he is a liar. For anyone who does not love his brother, whom he has seen, cannot love God, whom he has not seen. And he has given us this command: Whoever loves God must also love his brother.

Before everyone left for a quiet time, Tim asked the group to contemplate the following three questions:

1. What has God revealed about Himself in these verses?
2. What has God revealed to you about the most meaningful way you can express your love for Him in your relationships with your brothers and sisters in Christ?
3. How can you be different in your relationships with your brothers and sisters in Christ to better express your love for God?

After the quiet time, they reconvened in the main conference room. When Pastor Mike asked for volunteers to share what had become clear to them during their time of reflection, the theme of their remarks was almost universal. They spoke of realizing how far they had drifted away from connecting God's love for them as a guiding force in their relationships. They expressed excitement about the potential for renewing a missing dimension to their relationships and to the church.

Tim looked at the peaceful faces of his friends. It was as if all of them in some private way had reawakened some very special part of themselves. As a group, they seemed less guarded and self-conscious. The tension that had surrounded them a week ago had vanished, and something powerful had taken its place. For the first time, Tim sensed the presence of the Holy Spirit among them.

The final activity of the retreat involved the elders breaking into small groups to brainstorm how they could take their excitement back into the church. The goal was to develop a restoration plan with the ultimate goal of transforming Beacon Hill into the most loving place in town.

As the groups reported back, Tim wrote their best thinking on whiteboards and led them through a process that created a working plan for going forward over the months leading up to Beacon Hill's thirtieth anniversary celebration.

Among many ideas, the plan included the following:

- A presentation of the new "Most Loving Place in Town" vision to the congregation by Pastor Mike and Tim Manning

- A series of worship services and sermons by Pastor Mike focused on the nine components of love found in 1 Corinthians 13

- A six-week small group Bible study on putting the love of Jesus into action

- A special weekend set aside in all adult, student, and children's ministry classes for prayer and reflection on the teaching of Jesus on love, forgiveness, and reconciliation

♥ Regular times of prayer focused on restoring the love of God and one another in the heart of the congregation

Someone even suggested that Egos Anonymous meetings be held on a regular basis, especially before and after each congregational business meeting.

Tim and Mike were thrilled with the results of this meeting. Tim was particularly pleased with a suggestion that the wonderful book Clair mailed him, *The Greatest Thing in the World*, be required reading in each adult Sunday school class.

"I can't wait to develop marriage and parenting classes in love-based leadership," said Mike with a smile. "With all the good work we've been doing, I'm excited about sharing what we've been up to with the congregation. I think when we open this up to everyone, the expressions of love in relationships at Beacon Hill will rise dramatically."

"I totally agree," said Tim. "This isn't a plan we'll be delivering *to* the congregation; it's a plan we'll be executing *with* the congregation. If everyone owns a piece of the problem and gets involved in being part of the solution, our church is bound to become the most loving place in town."

Chapter 20

GATHERED IN HIS NAME

Pastor Mike looked out at the Beacon Hill congregation. As he had been doing regularly since returning from his sabbatical, he prayed a silent prayer that he could get his ego out of the way and communicate as clearly as possible God's love for His church. With a heart filled with love and excitement, he addressed the crowd.

"Good morning, and welcome to this new day in the life of Beacon Hill Community Church. Let us pray."

When he'd finished the opening prayer, Pastor Mike stepped out from behind the podium. He didn't want anything standing between him and his flock.

"My message this morning is going to be a little different

from what you are accustomed to hearing," he said. "I'm going to bring you up to speed on the miracles that have been happening behind the scenes here at Beacon Hill Community Church—things that are already impacting the life of the church. First, let me put your mind at ease. This is not going to be a surprise fund-raising appeal," he said with a smile.

With that opening, Pastor Mike shared with the congregation the letter about lost love that had started the church leaders' transformational journey. He told them about Dani, the young woman who'd left Beacon Hill because she'd been given the cold shoulder. He went on to relate the story of his meeting on the airplane with author Vince Blakely and how this well-known businessman had opened his eyes to the good news of Jesus' servant leadership mandate and role modeling.

"A week ago, Tim Manning called the Elder Council together, and we all did some soul-searching out at the YMCA conference center. Granted, it wasn't a five-star retreat," Pastor Mike joked, "but it was divine nevertheless." A wave of subdued laughter rippled through the crowd.

"On a serious note," he continued, "we wanted to see where we stacked up as loving servant leaders, so we conducted what we hope was a fearless inventory of our hearts. In the process, we uncovered some behavior and attitudes that we're not proud of, and we've sought God's forgiveness. We'll be asking for yours as well."

A new attentiveness showed in the faces of the congregation. People were sitting up straighter, and Pastor Mike felt all eyes were on him.

"We went to the Bible to see what Jesus had in mind for His church," he explained. "Using Jesus' thoughts as our guide, we've developed a vision statement for Beacon Hill Community Church. Simply put, we want to make this the most loving place in town. We've come to realize that all the programs, Bible studies, and outreach activities in the world will not honor God or profit us spiritually if our hearts are not in tune with the divine love of Jesus, and if we're not sharing that love with others."

Someone in the crowd shouted out, "Amen!"

Pastor Mike went on to describe the good work that had come out of the elders' retreat. He ended his talk by inviting the congregation to share their ideas and energy about how to make Beacon Hill the most loving place in town, and encouraging the change to begin with themselves.

Although the overall response to the vision that Pastor Mike presented to the church was highly favorable, it was not unanimous. Over the next few weeks, many people had questions to be answered, and several expressed fear and concern as they grappled with what specific changes they would have to make in their attitudes and behavior toward one another.

Forgiveness, apologies, and reconciliation flowed more freely than in the past—but not always and not in every relationship.

Pastor Mike kept the focus on the vision of a loving church in his weekly sermons. He encouraged the congregation by praising progress and confessing his ego challenges. In the past, rumors and misinformation had caused dissension. Now Tim and Pastor Mike used quarterly roundtable discussions with randomly selected members of the congregation to provide facts about matters of concern, which increased understanding and harmony. On the other hand, sometimes the church discovered that doing "the loving thing" required courage and a willingness to speak the truth, even at the risk of failure and rejection.

Just as Tim had predicted, the restoration really took off when church members began putting their ideas into action.

The thing that made the biggest difference was prayer. In a new and vibrant way, Beacon Hill Community Church embraced the words of Jesus: "My house will be called a house of prayer." Making Beacon Hill a house of prayer brought a new dimension to all activities and relationships. Prayer was expanded beyond personal "help me" and "thank you" requests. Pastor Mike led the congregation in rediscovering prayer as the most powerful resource that God gave to His community. People began to use prayer as their first response rather than as their last resort, praying to glorify God and invite Him into every dimension of their lives.

As the days and weeks went by, the focus at the church shifted. Rather than coming from a place of competitiveness, people acted from the knowledge of how much God loved everyone and wanted everyone to love one another. Attitudes started to change as people slowly began to get rid of their ego-centered ways of approaching problems and projects. Over time, people's behavior became more consistent with that of a loving community. There was a renewed feeling of trust among church members. It didn't happen all at once, and there were many bumps along the way.

As the bumps evened out, an amazing thing began to happen. Congregation members reported that the changes within Beacon Hill were spilling into their lives outside the church. Church members started to review their priorities in their marriages and families. They found that relearning the loving habits of patience, kindness, generosity, courtesy, humility, unselfishness, good temper, guilelessness, and sincerity provided a powerful antidote to the strain that busyness had placed on their relationships.

Some members described how they were applying the loving habits and the power of prayer they'd learned at Beacon Hill in their work relationships. As a result, church members' workplaces were becoming loving places as well.

Eventually the loving environment of Beacon Hill became noticeable to people in the community. Tim and Mike's proudest moment came on the day that Jerry, a longtime member of the congregation, reported something he'd heard in line at the local supermarket.

"A newcomer to town was telling someone she was looking

for a home church and asked for recommendations," Jerry said. "The guy she was talking to—an old veteran around town—said, 'Try Beacon Hill Community Church. I don't know too much about it, except that the people up there sure love one another.'"

ON A SUNNY Sunday in June of the following year, Pastor Mike had a proposition for the congregation.

"We've certainly improved our community outreach and good works," he said. "I'm proud to say that we have taken loving each other outside our walls and into the community. Now we have the opportunity to step up our generosity. We need you to lend your hearts, hands—and muscle!

"We're planning a trip to build homes for two great families who lost their houses in the downstate tornadoes last year. This four-day trip will be our opportunity to express the love of Jesus to one another as well as to those less fortunate than we are. We will be staying at our sister church in the area, which has offered to provide us with our meals and a place to sleep. Beacon Hill Community Church is donating money for building materials from our benevolence fund."

Even though the church had become a far more loving place in the past year, Pastor Mike had low expectations for participation in this event. Historically the congregation had a poor track record in outreach events. For these reasons,

Pastor Mike did not expect more than a handful of people to sign on.

"Can I see a show of hands to get a sense of how many of you might be interested?" he asked.

Pastor Mike could hardly believe his eyes. A sea of hands rose from the crowd. He smiled as he looked out at row upon row of faces smiling back. Then he saw something that nearly burst his heart with joy: Dani, the young woman who'd felt left out in the cold, was sitting in the back. As their eyes met, she smiled and raised her hand high in the air.

Chapter 21

LOVE ENDURES

The early morning air was still cool, but Tim knew that by noon the midsummer humidity would turn the building site into something closer to a sauna. The Beacon Hill Community Church building crew had started the second day on the job site early, and today they were seeing results. The foundation had been laid, the framing was up, most of the siding had been painted, and the walls were about to go on.

Tim looked across the building site, where the owners-to-be—a young couple with three redheaded kids aged nine, five, and two—were helping Pastor Mike and Rick Reardon haul the ridge vents and shingles that would be used for the roof. The painting crew had congregated at the rear of the lot, where Dani was leading a small chorus in a rousing rendition of "I've Been Working on the Railroad." Above the music Tim heard the sound of an engine approaching. Another vanload of church members was arriving to help out.

Tim stayed focused on the task before him, nailing sheathing to a framed wall lying on the ground. After he pounded in the last nail, he stood and shook the stiffness out of his knees. He leaned down and slipped his hands under the top edge of the wall, preparing to lift it upright. *Better bend my knees*, he thought. *This sucker's heavy.*

"Need some help with that?"

The voice was familiar, though he hadn't heard it in a long time. Tim looked over his shoulder and was startled to see the face of his old friend and nemesis, Gordy Phillips.

"Y-yeah," he stammered. "Thanks."

Gordy took hold of the wall, and together they hoisted it into place.

Pastor Mike looked over and called out, "Well done!"

Tim felt a surge of happiness. These were the words he'd always longed to hear. *Well done, good and faithful servant.*

"Thanks!" Tim shouted back. "Couldn't have done it without my buddy here!" He looked back at Gordy and smiled.

Gordy shrugged. "No biggie," he said. But there was a light in his eyes, and his smile was warm.

"Forgive me?" Tim asked.

"Done," said Gordy with a wave of his hand. "Ancient history. I've been a jerk too—sorry."

The tears that sprang to Tim's eyes took him by surprise. He bit his lip and stared at the ground, silently thanking God for His merciful, all-healing love. Where there once had been pain, now he felt joy. Where there once had been anger, now he felt tenderness. Where there once had been darkness, now he saw light.

The letter had promised that by restoring love to the church, he and Beacon Hill would receive blessings beyond his imagination. That promise was being fulfilled. Looking at his friend, Tim understood the profound wisdom of Jesus' command found in John 13:34:

"As I have loved you, so you must love one another."

Now he knew at the deepest level why, of all the things people could do, nothing was more important than to love God and love one another. Without love, human activity was meaningless.

Someone called out for another box of nails.

"Come on," Gordy said with a smile. "Let's go help these guys."

DISCUSSION GUIDE

This guide is designed to provide a starting point for readers of *The Most Loving Place in Town* to gain insight into themselves, their churches, and the loving relationships they enjoy with Jesus and with one another. Choose one or two discussion questions from each chapter, based upon the particular interest of your group, and open your hearts to the guidance of the Holy Spirit to teach you what you need to know and where to go next.

Enjoy the journey!

Chapter 1: The Letter

1. How would you describe Tim Manning's perspective on the health of the church and the success of his leadership at the beginning of the story?

2. What was the key difference between how the letter writer and Tim viewed the health of the church?

3. If you were in Tim's place, how and why would you have reacted differently to the contents of the letter he received?

4. What signs of the internal health of your home church are most likely to generate leadership action if they are moving in the wrong direction?

5. What do you think are most important to Jesus as indications of the spiritual health of your church? Please refer to Matthew 21:13; John 13:34–35; 17:20–24; and 21:15–17.

6. Discuss any differences or similarities between what drives leadership action in your church and those you define as most important to Jesus.

Chapter 2: The Phone Call

1. What effect did the phone call from Dani Wilson have on Tim Manning?

2. Describe the positive and negative elements of Dani's experience at Beacon Hill Community Church that led her to the conclusion it was not "the most loving place in town."

3. Describe the framework for providing effective feedback and encouragement that Tim noted when he reread the letter he had trashed.

4. Discuss what it means to be "under the guidance of the Holy Spirit."

Chapter 3: Love Lost

1. Name three positive steps that Tim took in response to the negative feedback he received about the church and his leadership.
2. Read Colossians 3:12–14:

> As God's chosen people, holy and dearly loved, clothe yourselves with compassion, kindness, humility, gentleness and patience. Bear with each other and forgive whatever grievances you may have against one another. Forgive as the Lord forgave you. And over all these virtues put on love, which binds them all together in perfect unity.

   A. Which aspects of love described in this passage are found in your local church?
   B. Which are most likely to be extended to others?
   C. Which are least likely to be extended to others?
3. What are the biggest barriers to and the biggest enhancers of the free flow of trust in your relationships within your local church community?

Chapter 4: Blind Spots Revealed

1. Describe the last time you spent a significant period alone with God.

2. How would you rate your prayer life today compared to two years ago?

   Hotter and more intense ___ Colder and less frequent ___

   About the same ___

   Explain.

3. When you take time to get into God's Word, how do you most often approach the Scriptures—as a way to enrich your relationship with Him or as a source of teaching material or validation of some position you have taken?

4. Read 1 John 4:11–12 and discuss how to stay in love with God's people:

   Dear friends, since God so loved us, we also ought to love one another. No one has ever seen God; but if we love one another, God lives in us and his love is made complete in us.

Chapter 5: A Rocking Chair Revelation

1. Read Matthew 18:3:

   I tell you the truth, unless you change and become like little children, you will never enter the kingdom of heaven.

Reflect on Tim's description of "how unrestrained and joyfully his little son had presumed and anticipated his love." What thoughts come to mind about your relationship and response to God's love?

2. Pause and reflect on how you would answer the question Tim posed to himself: "He wondered whether he was approaching God in the same way or whether he was holding back or lacking trust."

3. Describe the last time you felt God's unconditional love in your life.

4. How would you respond to the view that you and all the people you have met or will ever meet are the objects of God's unconditional affection?

Chapter 6: A Bedside Blessing

1. Select something you would like to see changed in the life of your church. Do the multiple "I want to . . . so that _____" exercise, and discuss your motives and results.

2. Discuss how the statement "Right causes do not guarantee good motives" applies within a church setting.

3. Read James 4:2–3:

You do not have, because you do not ask God. When you ask, you do not receive, because you ask with wrong motives, that you may spend what you get on your pleasures.

What questions does this passage raise about why things prayed for with great passion may not be answered in the way we want or in the way we expect?

4. Discuss how the following statements taken from Matthew 5:3–6 apply to restoring a love relationship that has grown cold:

- ♥ Blessed are the poor in spirit.

- ♥ Blessed are those who mourn.

- ♥ Blessed are the meek.

- ♥ Blessed are those who hunger and thirst for righteousness.

Chapter 7: Forgiven Much, Love More

1. What three pieces of evidence would you cite as proof that God loves you?

2. What three pieces of evidence would you cite as proof that you love God?

3. Discuss the challenge of "admitting I'm broken and letting God do the fixing."

4. Write your own Father's Day card for today and share its content.

Chapter 8: A Roadblock to Love

1. List four things that brothers and sisters in Christ owe one another.

2. List four more things that colaborers in the life of the church owe one another.

3. List four additional things that members of the same body with different responsibilities as followers and leaders owe one another.

4. Discuss a time when encouragement from an unsuspecting source made a difference in your life.

Chapter 9: Reaching Out

1. Describe the ego challenges that Tim had to overcome before he could reach out to Gordy Phillips. What resources did he use to overcome these barriers?

2. Describe the new challenges Tim faced when Gordy rejected his attempt at reconciliation. What resources did Tim employ to respond to the rejection he experienced?

3. Discuss a time when you experienced the "secondhand smoke" fallout from someone else's unforgiving spirit. Describe the impact on your relationships.

4. Define the difference between *forgiving* and *forgetting*. Which are we called on to do with the help of the Holy Spirit? What are the consequences if we don't? See Matthew 6:14–15 for guidance.

Chapter 10: Finding Self-Worth

1. Why is forgiving yourself harder than forgiving others?
2. Name three barriers to forgiveness.
3. Who suffers when forgiveness is withheld?
4. Describe the connection between our forgiveness of others and our relationship with God.

Chapter 11: Building His Church

1. It was clear to Pastor Mike that the church Jesus had in mind was not limited to a building or an organizational structure. Describe and discuss the most important characteristic of Jesus' church.
2. Place the name of your church at the beginning of each of the following statements. Assess the current internal life of your church based on each of the characteristics of the church Jesus had in mind. If your answer is positive, describe what keeps things moving in the right direction. If your answer is negative, discuss one thing that might turn things in the right direction.

   A. _____ is a church where love is the distinctive internal characteristic that guides lives and relationships.

   True _____ False _____

   B. _____ is a community of interdependent people that is unified by love.

   True _____ False _____

C. _____ is a church that readily accesses all the spiritual resources it requires to fulfill its mission.

    True _____ False _____

D. _____ is a church where prayer is the most distinctive practice.

    True _____ False _____

E. _____ is a church that relies on the Holy Spirit to guide and direct its course of action.

    True _____ False _____

F. _____ is a church that bears much fruit by abiding in Christ.

    True _____ False _____

Chapter 12: A Chance Encounter?

1. Read Matthew 20:25–28:

> Jesus called them together and said, "You know that the rulers of the Gentiles lord it over them, and their high officials exercise authority over them. Not so with you. Instead, whoever wants to become great among you must be your servant, and whoever wants to be first must be your slave—just as the Son of Man did not come to be served, but to serve, and to give his life as a ransom for many."

A. Describe what Jesus mandated to His followers as the key distinction of how they were to consider leadership in their relationship to one another.

B. Describe the basic question that followers of Jesus must answer in each situation where they have an opportunity to influence the thinking, actions, or development of another person: Am I seeking to _____ or be _____?

2. Place a check mark next to the following words that best describe your usual reaction to negative feedback about your leadership and an X next to the words that best describe your reaction to positive feedback:

____ Fear   ____ Curiosity

____ Anger   ____ Gratitude

____ Denial   ____ Surprise

____ Sadness   ____ Discouragement

What is the root cause for any differences between your responses to negative and positive feedback?

3. Describe and assess the effectiveness of efforts by the leaders in your church to prepare their successors.

Chapter 13: The Leader Jesus Had in Mind

1. As Mike dove into the Gospels, he realized that there were two parts to the servant leadership Jesus had in mind. What were they?

2. A compelling vision tells people who they are, where they are going, and what will guide their journey.

   A. In Matthew 4:19, Jesus told His disciples He would make them "fishers of men." What does this tell us about who Jesus wants us to be?

   B. In Mathew 28:19, Jesus asked His disciples to "go and make disciples of all nations, baptizing them in the name of the Father and of the Son and of the Holy Spirit." What does this tell us about where Jesus envisioned His church going?

   C. In John 13:34, Jesus was clear about the operating value that was the top priority for His church. What was that value?

3. Describe the vision you would like to have for your local church.

   A. How will you communicate that vision to the congregation and wider community?

   B. How will you sustain people's passion and commitment to that vision?

4. Pastor Mike realized that the traditional hierarchy is good for the visionary aspect of leadership but that successful implementation requires turning the hierarchy upside down and putting the leader at the bottom, serving those with the responsibility to manifest the vision.

   A. What would it look like if your church turned the leadership pyramid upside down for the implementation phase of the church's vision?

B. What new actions by your church's leaders would have the greatest impact on enhancing people's commitment to the vision?

Chapter 14: A Meeting of Hearts and Minds

1. What would have been the result if either Tim Manning or Mike Reston had given in to the fear factor in their relationship?
2. How did Mike's and Tim's mutual prayers set the stage for moving ahead with a common spirit?
3. What did Mike and Tim start to build between them with their openness and humility as a foundation for moving forward?
4. Read John 15:5:

   "I am the vine; you are the branches. If a man remains in me and I in him, he will bear much fruit; apart from me you can do nothing."

   Pause and reflect on the implications of the word *nothing* in this passage. How do Mike and Tim need to proceed if they are going to fulfill their mission?

Chapter 15: Love-Based Leadership

1. How consistently do leaders of your church, including yourself, reflect the following characteristics of the leadership Jesus had in mind for His church?

   A. Servant leaders grounded in His unconditional and eternal purpose of glorifying God the Father.

   Almost always _____ Sometimes _____ Rarely _____

   B. Leaders lovingly committed to and involved in the nurturing and care of both the weak and mature members of His church.

   Almost always _____ Sometimes _____ Rarely _____

   C. Leaders who display God-grounded confidence and humility.

   Almost always _____ Sometimes _____ Rarely _____

   D. Leaders who actively model and teach servant leadership to future generations.

   Almost always _____ Sometimes _____ Rarely _____

   E. Leaders who have been transformed by the Holy Spirit.

   Almost always _____ Sometimes _____ Rarely _____

2. Select one leadership characteristic you rated as *Sometimes* or *Rarely* that, if improved to *Almost always*, would have the most significant impact in your church. Discuss how this change would help your church become the most loving place in town.

Chapter 16: The Challenge of Change

1. Pause and reflect on the following elements of effective change and the supreme example and promises of Jesus.

   A. Lasting change starts with clear goals and direction.

   "For God so loved the world that he gave his one and only Son, that whoever believes in him shall not perish but have eternal life. For God did not send his Son into the world to condemn the world, but to save the world through him."

   —John 3:16–17

   B. To accept the need for change, people have to know that you are personally committed and will make sacrifices too.

   "Greater love has no one than this, that he lay down his life for his friends."

   —John 15:13

   C. As a change leader, you don't have to do it all on your own.

   "If you love me, you will obey what I command. And I will ask the Father, and he will give you another Counselor to be with you forever."

   —John 14:15–16

D. Effective change is more about the journey than announcing the destination.

"Therefore go and make disciples of all nations, baptizing them in the name of the Father and of the Son and of the Holy Spirit, and teaching them to obey everything I have commanded you. And surely I am with you always, to the very end of the age."
—Matthew 28:19–20

2. Why is it important to hear people's concerns about change?
3. Discuss how the fear and pride of church leaders might get in the way of necessary change. How might an Egos Anonymous meeting help leaders move beyond ego issues and embrace positive change?

Chapter 17: Love Revealed

1. Consider each of the nine components of love: patience, kindness, generosity, humility, courtesy, unselfishness, good temper, guilelessness, and sincerity.
   A. Which three components of love are most meaningful to you?
   B. Which three are hardest for you to express or demonstrate on a regular basis?

C. Which three are most evident in the life of your church?

D. Which three are most lacking in the life of your church?

2. With your answers in mind, what would a prayer in the spirit of Philippians 4:6–7 contain?

Do not be anxious about anything, but in everything, by prayer and petition, with thanksgiving, present your requests to God. And the peace of God, which transcends all understanding, will guard your hearts and your minds in Christ Jesus.

Chapter 18: Calling in the Elders

1. The Beacon Hill Community Church elders listed things they were going to have to give up to take the lead in making their church the most loving place in town. Their list included holding grudges, regarding busyness as a badge of honor, using church attendance as part of a good person to-do list, judging others, being insincere in dealing with the needs and cares of others, and acting as a performance critic. What would you, as a leader in your church, add to the list?

2. Discuss one area that other people might like you to work on first. What reason would you give for your response?

3. What are your biggest barriers to making the changes required? What is the first step you would need to take to overcome one of these barriers?

4. What resources do you have as a follower of Jesus that will be most helpful in making the changes you listed?

Chapter 19: Taking Inventory

1. What would happen to the internal environment of your church today if, as one of the Beacon Hill elders remarked, "We have to search our hearts, heads, hands, and habits, and find ways to make the 'loving thing' our single leadership priority"?

2. The first step to restoration of the love priority for followers of Jesus is "owning up to the problem" of putting other things in the place that only the love of God and one another should occupy in their lives. Pause and reflect: What are some good things involved in church life that can slowly edge out the love of God and one another?

3. Each thing you just listed may be hard to put back into its proper place in your life and in the life of your church. These things may currently be central to what you believe it means to be a faithful follower of Jesus. What will be your greatest need and greatest fear in making the change required to put love of God into action by loving His people?

4. Which of God's promises are most meaningful to you as you consider owning your part of the problem and uniting with others in making your church the most loving place in your town?

Chapter 20: Gathered in His Name

1. What do you think the response would be if your pastor and leadership team came before the congregation with the vision of making your church the most loving place in town?

2. What three questions would you want answered before you signed up to be a willing and active participant in making the changes needed to accomplish the new vision for your church?

3. To make prayer the most potent element in the change process, how would the way your church prays as a body have to change?

4. What is one specific idea that you would like to see put into action as a positive step in making your church the most loving place in town?

Chapter 21: Love Endures

1. Discuss the power of repentance, authentic apology, and forgiveness in restoring loving relationships.

2. Is there someone you need to forgive? If the answer is yes, what first step can you take to make this a reality?

3. Is there someone to whom you need to deliver an authentic apology? If the answer is yes, what could you do today to begin the process?

4. Is there some hidden bitterness or anger you need to lay at the foot of the cross? If the answer is yes, take a few moments and offer a prayer to God about your bitterness or anger.

TAKE THE FIRST step in any of these areas and you will glorify God. You could very well start a movement to make your church the most loving place in town.

We would love to know the story of your church and its journey to becoming the most loving place in town. E-mail us at MLPStories@LeadLikeJesus.com.

ABOUT THE AUTHORS

KEN BLANCHARD, coauthor of *The One Minute Manager*® and more than forty other management and leadership books, is universally characterized as one of the most insightful, powerful, and compassionate people in business today. He is known for his knack for making the seemingly complex easy to understand. Ken is chief spiritual officer of The Ken Blanchard Companies™, a global leader in workplace learning, employee productivity, leadership, and team effectiveness. Along with Phil Hodges, he is the cofounder of Lead Like Jesus, a ministry founded in 1999 to help leaders from all walks of life explore and express the leadership principles Jesus lived.

PHIL HODGES, a lifelong friend of Ken Blanchard, served as a human resource and industrial relations manager in corporate America for thirty-six years and as member and chairman of his local church elder council for more than ten years. Phil finds his greatest joy in life as a husband, father, and grandpa. In 1999, Ken and Phil cofounded Lead Like Jesus, where he serves as chief content officer. He is the coauthor of three books: *Leadership by the Book* with Ken Blanchard and Bill Hybels, *The Servant Leader* with Ken Blanchard, and *Lead Like Jesus* with Ken Blanchard.

CREATING THE MOST LOVING PLACE IN TOWN
INCLUDES DEVELOPING LEADERS
WHO LEAD LIKE JESUS!

FREE ONLINE LEADERSHIP TRAINING

Whether you're a pastor, a nursery worker, a parking lot attendee, or a new member, you have influence over those who visit or attend your church. At Lead Like Jesus, we believe that everyone is a leader and must develop and steward the influence he or she has been given.

We would like to introduce you to the greatest leadership model who ever lived. As believers, we've been challenged throughout our journey of faith to emulate the behaviors and ways of Jesus. But we seldom recognize His leadership genius. At Lead Like Jesus, we believe that Jesus is the greatest leadership model who ever lived, and that leading like Jesus will bring a leadership revolution and change our world as we know it. We must live the model we want the world to become!

We want to help you maximize your leadership and invite you to enroll in a FREE online leadership training course today. Learn leadership lessons from the master and make the most of your opportunities as you learn to lead like Jesus!

THE LEAD LIKE JESUS JOURNEY

STEP 1 : Read *The Most Loving Place in Town*

STEP 2 : Sign Up for the FREE Lead Like Jesus Training Course
www.LeadLikeJesus.com/leadershiptraining

Modules Include:
- Leadership 101
- The Greatest Leadership Model of All Time
- Maximizing Your Influence
- Staying on Top of Your Game

STEP 3 : Answer Online Questions for Each Module

STEP 4 : Request Your Lead Like Jesus Training e-Certificate

LEAD LIKE JESUS

ALSO FROM
LEAD LIKE JESUS...

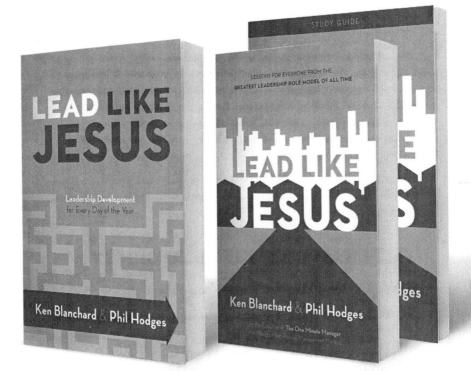

Learn More About Lead Like Jesus Resources and Events at www.LeadLikeJesus.com

LEAD LIKE JESUS